P9-DGC-129

A DOG OWNER'S GUIDE TO

Standard, Miniature & Toy

POODLES

Tetra●Press

No. 16024

A DOG OWNER'S GUIDE TO

Standard, Miniature & Toy

POODLES

Jackie Ransom

Photographs by Marc Henrie

A Salamander Book

© 1987 Salamander Books Ltd.,
Published in the USA by
Tetra Press,
201 Tabor Road,
Morris Plains,
N.J. 07950

ISBN 3-923880-63-4

Credits

Editor: Jo Finnis Designer: Philip Gorton
Photographs: Marc Henrie, Sally Anne Thompson (pp 81, 109, back
cover); Douglas Ransom (pp 79, 102)
Illustrations: Ray Hutchins
Color origination: Bantam Litho Ltd
Typesetting: The Old Mill
Printed in Portugal by Printer Portuguesa

Contents

Foreword

I have had the pleasure of owning Poodles for more than thirty
years. I have bred them, shown them and delighted in their
company. During that time I have read many books about them —
some were historical reference books; some were practical, do-it-
yourself clipping manuals.
This book by Jackie Ransom is a refreshing change. The author
has a wide appreciation and knowledge of dogs in general, and this
is evident in her chapters on the general care of the puppy and the
adult dog, and the world of dog shows. Anyone who is thinking of
acquiring a Poodle as a pet or to show, anyone who already has
one and even Poodle 'addicts' of long-standing, should find this
book interesting and informative. She has presented her facts in a
readable style blended with an obvious understanding and love of
her subject.
I have enjoyed reading the book and I am sure you will too. I
advise you to start straight away . . .
Daphne MacDougall

636.76
Ran

45900

Author

Jackie Ransom has bred many top-winning Poodles and is a member of the
Kennel Club and The Breed Standards And Stud Book Committee in the
United Kingdom. She has written many articles for various magazines
worldwide, and has contributed the Breed Notes to 'Dog World', a top-
selling dog paper in the UK, since 1974.
Since her first judging appointment in 1965, Jackie quickly found herself in
demand to judge both in the UK and many other countries. She has judged
at Crufts Dog Show several times, and has been passed by the Kennel
Club to judge the Toy Group. She also awards Challenge Certificates to
breeds in the Working and Utility Groups.
Jackie has also established an enviable record in breeding, showing and
judging the Bichon Frisé.
She lives in Wembley Park, near London, where she has a splendid library
of historical dog publications, cards and prints.

Contributor

Keith Butt, MA, VetMB(Cantab), MRCVS has contributed the chapter on
Veterinary Care. Keith qualified in 1961 at Cambridge University. He runs
his own veterinary practice in Kensington, London, and is himself a breeder
and owner of many different breeds of pedigree dogs.

US consultant

Hal Sundstrom, as president of Halamar Inc, publishers of North Virginia,
has been editing and publishing magazines on travel and pure-bred dogs
since 1972. He is the recipient of six national writing and public excellent
awards from the Dog Writer's Association of America, of which he is now
president, and he is a past president of the Collie Club of America.
Hal has an extensive background and enormous experience in the dog
world as a breeder/handler/exhibitor, match and sweeps judge, officer and
director of specialty and all-breed clubs, show and symposium chairman,
and officer of the Arizona and Hawaii Councils of Dog Clubs.

Photographer

Marc Henrie began his career as a Stills Man at the famous Ealing Film
Studios in London. He then moved to Hollywood where he worked for
MGM, RKO, Paramount and Warner Brothers, photographing the
Hollywood greats: Humphrey Bogart, Edward G Robinson, Gary Cooper,
Joan Crawford and Ingrid Bergman, to name a few. He was one of the last
photographers to photograph Marilyn Monroe. During this time, he was in
great demand to photograph the stars with their pets.
Later, after he had returned to England, Marc specialized in photographing
dogs and cats, rapidly establishing an international reputation.
He has won numerous photographic awards, most recently the Kodak
Award for the Best Animal Photograph and the Neal Foundation Award for
Outstanding Photography of Animal Behaviour.
Marc is married to ex-ballet dancer, Fiona Henrie, who now writes and
illustrates books on animals. They live in West London with their daughter
Fleur, two King Charles Cavalier Spaniels and a cat called Topaz.

Author's acknowledgements

The author wishes to thank Marjorie Ransom for typing the manuscript;
Gordon Davis, Manager of the Awards Department and Ian Logan,
Manager of the Registration Department at The Kennel Club for their
invaluable help.

Introduction

In writing this book on Poodles, I will endeavour to answer the numerous questions raised by prospective owners who have yet to experience the great pleasure to be enjoyed from this intelligent, amusing, loyal and elegant dog, as well as to extend current owners' knowledge of their breed. The three varieties — the Standard, Miniature and Toy — each have their special charm, with a marvellous choice of colours: Black, White, Brown, Apricot, Silver and Cream.

Trends in popularity

The popularity of the Miniature and Toy Poodles reached its peak in the early 1960s as shown by the registrations at the Kennel Club of Great Britain and the American Kennel Club, whose records are the most comprehensive guide to the popularity of any pedigree dog. In the UK during 1960, the number of Miniature Poodles recorded reached an all time high: over 23,000, while the Toy Poodle registrations were just over 9,000. The Standard Poodle, however, had slightly declined; the number of registrations in the same year amounted to 436 as against 527 in 1957. Over the last 26 years, both the Miniature and Toy have steadily decreased, and stood at 1,233 and 2,166 in 1986.

In the United States from 1900 up to 1935, the Poodle was not popular being considered by most as a useless animal. This attitude changed completely with the importation from England of the Swiss bred White Standard, Int Ch Nunsoe Duc de la Terrace of Blakeen (imported, owned and handled by Mrs Sherman Hoyt), who distinguished himself by being the first Poodle to win Best in Show at the prestigious Westminster Kennel Club Show in 1935. From that

Left: *Ch Vicmars Devil in Demand, owned by Ann Penfold, showing the perfection of Poodles presented for exhibition today.*

Above: *A pre-20th century Corded Poodle, 'Ronto', owned by a Mrs Gibbs. Any Poodle coat will cord if left long and ungroomed.*

time onwards, the breed's popularity increased with the Miniature gaining favour over the Standard, reaching its peak in the 1960s as the most popular breed in the United States. Now in the 1980s, while no longer quite so popular, the breed's three sizes are still firm favourites.

Any great popularity for a breed invariably brings with it commercialism, as was the case up to 1962. This resulted in many litters being bred without thought or consideration, thereby producing puppies quite unworthy of the name Poodle. The present day Miniatures and Toys in both the US and the UK are practically guaranteed to be bred with great care and consideration by dedicated breeders who, from past experience and knowledge, raise their puppies to become healthy, happy and stable companions — Poodles which are a pleasure to own.

The Standard is rising

The Standard Poodle has never been a commercial proposition, hence its slow but steady rise in popularity in the UK since the 1960s. In 1986, the number registered stood at 1,103. This increase I feel is due to the very much improved presentation both in and out of the show ring. With the equally improved overall conformation and elegance, and the present day popularity of the larger breeds, the Standard Poodle is set to become even more popular.

Chapter One

A HISTORY OF THE POODLE

Origins
Introduction into England
Classification
The United States

The origin of the Poodle has been described many times over, proving its very ancient lineage. The first record of the breed was made by a friend of Dr Caius, the Swiss naturalist Conrad Gesner, in 1555. But it does seem likely that the ancients knew the breed also, since little Poodles were depicted on monuments erected during the reign of Emperor Augustus who died in 14 AD.

An excerpt from Vero Shaw's rare 'Book of the Dog', published in 1890, contributed by a Mr T H Joyce, a great admirer of the Poodle, gives a clear and concise outline of the breed's temperament, character and history as assessed in the 19th century. His account also serves to prove how little this breed has altered in what is now nearly 100 years.

The canine performer

'In England the Poodle proper is the least understood, and consequently the least appreciated, of almost any known breed of dog. Indeed, he is looked upon with a feeling approaching contempt, as a canine mountebank, amusing enough in his way like a "plum pudding" trick horse in a circus, but of no practical use in real life. And yet in a great measure those very characteristics which render him first and foremost among canine performers are due to the simple fact that he is far superior in intelligence to his fellows, and capable of acquiring a greater variety of accomplishments, from walking about on his hind-legs with a parasol and petticoats, to retrieving on land or in water; while it should not be forgotten that so great an authority as Sir Edwin Landseer, 1802-73, painted him as the type of Wisdom in "Laying Down the Law". In fact, in Germany, and indeed throughout a great portion of Northern Europe, he is looked upon as every whit as useful a companion as he is ornamental. He is also used for shooting purposes, as he is a capital water-dog, is easy to train either to retrieve or point, a steady and willing worker, moreover, and when well trained is extremely

---

Below: *A curly Standard Poodle painted by George Rankin in the late 1800s. Note the short mane, bare rib cage and loin.*

Cannon Hill Beauty.

Above: *Lady Di Huddlestone's 'Mossoo' born in 1877 in Paris, clipped to show 'the satin and astrakan coat to perfection'. From 'Stonehenge', 4th edition.*

Above right: *Ch Cannon Hill Beauty, a Black corded bitch sired by The Die Ex Garce Darling, born 1896, was still winning 1st prizes at ten years of age.*

Below: *'Monsieur's' photograph was used for an early 1900s' postcard, so somebody must have considered him attractive. We have come a long way since then in the art of presentation.*

tractable, and it is this quality of extreme docility which makes him a most valuable dog in the house, as he is full of fun, ever ready for a romp with a child or to fetch his master's slippers. He is also a capital watch-dog.

'Marvellous anecdotes, far too numerous to mention here, are told of the Poodle's faithfulness, affection, and versatile talent, ranging from the celebrated Munito who, in 1818, astonished all Paris by his clever card and arithmetical tricks; or the once well-known Paris Poodle of the Pont Neuf who used to dirty the boots of passers-by in order that his master — a shoeblack

Above: *Ch Stillington Jeremie, a Standard born 1932, exemplifies the 1930s' style of show trim in the Continental Lion Clip.*

Above: *Littleist of Eathorpe, a black Miniature born 1930, sired by Ch Spriggan Bell, shows the English Saddle Clip.*

— might have the benefit of cleaning them; to a white Poodle who, snubbed by his lady-love, committed suicide at Queenstown a few years since. Like a child, however, he requires careful handling, for while he is very easily trained, he is exceptionally sensitive, and is far more efficiently taught when treated rather as a sensible being than as an animal.

Origins
'The history of the Poodle and the details of his lineage are somewhat obscure. That he is of German origin there is no doubt, the name being identical in both languages — Pudel — and he, there, is ordinarily classed as the *Canis Familiaris Aquaticus,* being very closely allied to the more crisp and curly-haired water-fowl dog well known to our sportsmen of the marshes. He assuredly dates his existence from some centuries since, for in various illuminated manuscripts of the 16th century, and notably in one depicting an episode in the life of Margaret of York, the third wife of Charles the Bold of Burgundy, and in another representing a family group of Maximilian of Austria and his wife and child ('The Abridged Chronicles of Burgundy'), there is certainly the portrait of a shaven dog, which, allowing for the artistic shortcomings of that period, closely resembles the Poodle of the present

day. Again, in Martin de Vos' (1541-1603) picture of ''Tobit and His Dog'', which also dates from the 16th century, the faithful animal is an unmistakable shaven Poodle, while in the series of paintings of the story of ''Patient Griselda'' by Pinturicchio (1454-1513) in the National Gallery, a small shaven Poodle is conspicuous amongst the various spectators of Griselda's vicissitudes of fortune. At the present day the Poodle is found throughout Europe from Amsterdam to Naples, where, completely shaven, he may be seen taking his siesta under the shadow of some friendly wall or doorway.

Introduction into England
'The Poodle appears to have been introduced into England during the Continental Wars at the beginning of the century (*19th*), although performing dogs were known previous to this era; but he was a favourite in France long before that date, and in a fashion plate of the time of Louis XVI he is represented, shaven and shorn, begging hard for a biscuit from a child of the period.'

The Corded Poodle
At the end of the 19th century, most Standard Poodles in Great Britain were of the Corded variety. The first English Standard Poodle Champion (1890), Champion Achilles, was 23in (58.5cm) high

with cords measuring 30in (76cm) in length. The last entry for Corded Poodles was in the Kennel Club Stud Book for 1923; only two were listed. It is now considered that any Poodle coat will show a tendency to cord if left long and ungroomed.

Classification

In the UK, prior to 1910, Poodles under 15in (38cm) were classified with the Standards. From 1921 they were re-classified as Miniatures and entered under the Toy Group where they remained for three years. They were then re-classified in the Non-Sporting group with the Standards and the Toy Poodles, first

recognised by the KC in 1953.

The United States

As long ago as the 1880's, Poodles were known and exhibited in the US, mainly on the East Coast where several kennels imported both Standards and Miniatures from the UK and other parts of Europe. However, the large size was the most popular. The English Kennel Club Breed Standard and the American Kennel Club Standard were identical at that time; therefore both sizes and all colours were recognised. Today the American Standard differs very little from its English counterpart (see Chapter Seven). The American Toy Poodle must, however, be under 10in (25.5cm) and is shown in the Toy Group, while the Standard and Miniature are shown in the Non-Sporting Group.

Below: *A superb Toy, Ch Fabuleux Isn't She Gorgeous, owned by Mrs Anne Evans, England, shows the modern English Saddle Clip.*

Chapter Two

THE POODLE PUPPY

Choosing a puppy
Care of the puppy
Feeding
Training
Home health care

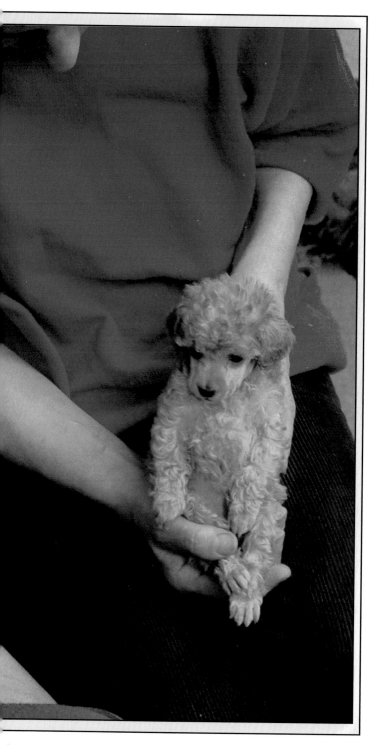

CHOOSING A PUPPY

It must not be forgotten that a dog is a living creature which, as a young puppy, requires as much care and consideration as a young child.

Sizes

As we already know, the Poodle comes in three sizes: the Standard over 15in (38cm), usually about 22in (56cm) at the shoulder; the Miniature under 15in (38cm) but over 11in (28cm) at the shoulder; the Toy under 11in (28cm).

A choice should be made according to your lifestyle. The Standard Poodle requires quite a lot of exercise and is certainly happier in country surroundings with plenty of opportunity for long walks, and where it can occasionally be allowed to run free. The Miniature will be quite content with daily walks and a fairly large garden, whereas the Toy is ideal for anyone with a small home and garden, or for the flat dweller who enjoys a walk to the park on good days.

Colours

The choice of colour is purely a matter of personal preference. I have often been asked whether the coat colour of the Poodle makes a difference to their temperament. From my own experience, I would say none at all; they are all delightful. A white coat will naturally require a little more care than the others, but all require a daily grooming to keep their coats smart and free from mats. It is also worth noting that although the Poodle does not shed its coat, it does require a visit to a canine beautician at least every six to eight weeks, an added expense which must be considered. If, however, you are prepared to learn the art of grooming and clipping your Poodle yourself, the detailed instructions and accompanying photographs in Chapter Four will be of great assistance. Do not expect to be able to achieve success quickly; both time and much patience is

required. If you can master the art of transforming a scruffy looking Poodle into a smart, well-presented one, you will enjoy a most rewarding experience.

Sex

Whichever sex you choose is also a matter of personal preference. In my opinion there is very little difference in temperament between the sexes in Poodles. Both the dog and the bitch are equal in intelligence and companionship. However, it is thought that a dog can be slightly more difficult to house train, whereas a bitch comes into season twice a year when she will be an attraction to most males in the near vicinity. This can be a nuisance, especially if you live in a densely-populated area. If you decide to have your bitch spayed, provided it is done early in life, this will not alter either her temperament or character. Neither will she get fat, if not overfed.

Above: *The three sizes, ranging from the Standard (usually 22in/56cm at the shoulder) to the Toy (under 11in/28cm).*

Below: *The Poodle comes in a variety of colours — from left to right: White, Apricot, Black, Cream, Silver and Brown.*

Kennels

Before buying your puppy, make as many enquiries as possible to make sure you buy from a breeder of good repute known for producing sound and healthy Poodles. Such names can be obtained from your kennel club (addresses listed at the back of the book) or from your local Poodle club. In the US, your local all-breed club will be able to supply details of reputable breeders. There are two dog papers published each week in the UK, 'Dog World' and 'Our Dogs' and one monthly, 'Dogs Monthly', available from your newsagent. In the US, 'Dog World' is published monthly, while two other magazines 'Pure Bred Dogs' and the 'American Kennel Gazette' are available by subscription from the American Kennel Club. These publications give notice of puppies for sale. Beware of kennels producing puppies for purely commercial reasons.

Having decided which size and colour you prefer, you should visit a kennel specialising in your choice. Any reputable breeder will probably allow you to see the puppies' mother, which will enable you to get some idea of how the puppy will look on maturity, especially if you are looking for a Silver or Apricot. Black, White and Brown Poodles are born pure black, white or brown, but Apricots need to be a deep colour when young as they fade somewhat on maturity. Silvers are born black but start turning silver on their feet and around the eyes quite soon after birth. You should, by eight weeks, get some idea of the final shade the Poodle will be at 18 months, but seeing the mother will give you an even better idea. Standard, Miniature and Toy Poodles can safely be purchased at eight weeks of age but not earlier.

Never hesitate to ask questions of the breeder, no matter how insignificant you may think your questions are. Most breeders will welcome your interest.

Below: *Making a choice between two attractive puppies, such as these, can be difficult for the prospective owner.*

Above: *An attractive litter looking alert and interested in the proceedings. Note their rich colour, black noses and dark eyes.*

Selecting an individual

In choosing your puppy, remember that Standard Poodles take far longer than either a Toy or Miniature to mature. Toys at eight weeks appear quite steady, the Miniature still a little unsteady at times, whereas the Standard appears quite awkward, with an ambling gait, looking overall rather like a young foal.

When choosing a puppy from a litter, try not to be tempted by the shy, retiring individual usually huddled in a corner, for whom you will undoubtedly feel sorry. Choose instead the happy bouncing extrovert who is obviously full of life.

You then need to make a closer examination of the puppy. Check the puppy's ears; they should be clean and pink without any odour. Any sign of brown discharge could indicate the presence of ear mites. Look for a clean mouth with white teeth, and eyes that are clear and bright. Run your fingers through the coat which should look and feel clean and healthy. Finally, check that the nails are short and neat, with dew claws removed.

Diet sheet

Having selected your puppy, it is wise to obtain from the breeder a diet sheet, detailing the quantities, type of food and the hours at which the puppy has become accustomed to being fed. If you can keep to the same times and diet for the first few days, this will reduce the chance of an upset stomach. Also, make a note of the dates when the puppy was wormed.

Papers

Finally, a receipt with the puppy's pedigree and, if required, the Kennel Club registration papers should be obtained at the time of purchase. The registration papers will consist of either an application form to register the dog, which you then complete and send to your Kennel Club with the appropriate fee; or a registration certificate, where the dog has already been named by the breeder but owner-ship needs to be transferred to you.

CARE OF THE PUPPY

The success of the new arrival in the family depends completely on the owner's preparation and early training of the puppy. Puppies, like children, must be taught from a very early age what is expected of them.

Equipment
You will need to make certain preparations for the puppy's arrival in its new home. For its bed, a strong cardboard box (large or small depending on the size of the puppy) with the front cut down is a better idea than a basket. Young puppies will chew anything when they are teething. A cardboard box,

Below: *A temporary bed for a young puppy — draught-proof, warm, cosy and easily-replaced when chewed or dirty. Make sure the box is free of staples.*

without any dangerous staples, can be renewed as necessary. When the puppy has passed the chewing stage, you can safely purchase a permanent basket or bed from a pet store. Fill the box with a soft, woolly blanket, vet-bed or soft cushion and place in a warm, draught-proof corner out of the family's way.

You will require a feeding bowl with a solid base, and a water bowl. Make sure the latter is full of fresh water at all times, and in a safe place.

Although very young Poodle puppies do not require much combing and brushing, it is a good idea to get them used to the comb and brush early and to stand still during the operation. For this, a steel comb and a wire brush are necessary (see Chapter Four on grooming). When older, a daily grooming is essential to keep the coat in good condition.

Although puppies must not be taken out into the street on a lead

Above: *These are all safe toys of the right size for even the youngest puppy. Nothing can be splintered and the soft toy is free from dangerous appendages.*

Above: *Tennis balls fray when chewed, plastic toys will splinter, the soft toy's eyes can be swallowed and large balls can lodge in the mouth.*

until fully inoculated, a small, soft collar and lead for a Miniature or Toy, and a leather collar and lead for a standard can be used to train the puppy in the garden. For road walks, however, a strong collar and lead are necessary. Dogs should always be exercised on a lead in built-up areas.

Toys can be anything you choose, but make sure they are safe toys without any dangerous appendages. They should all be too large for the puppy's mouth, otherwise they could become lodged in the mouth or throat causing great discomfort. Nylon tights or stockings knotted together several times make a very acceptable plaything.

Socialization and safety
On the puppy's first arrival at your home, everything will be strange and slightly awesome. Up until this time, the puppy will have had the constant companionship of his litter mates, and will be completely unused to being on its own. But the puppy will quickly adapt and respond to the warmth and companionship of its new home and owner.

From the first, the puppy must be taught that what you say is absolute law. If the dog disobeys, do not smack it, but use a very stern tone of voice whilst admonishing.

Remember that young puppies are used to being on the level and will fall if left on a chair or table. Always keep a firm hand on the puppy. Pick it up underneath its tummy holding its front legs from the outside with your thumb and second finger, placing your first finger between the legs. This way, with the puppy's body tucked under your arm, it will not be able to leap out of your hands and fall. Young children should only be allowed to hold the puppy while they are sitting on the floor. Take special care when opening and shutting doors; puppies are very quick and it is easy to catch their feet.

Make sure all electrical plugs and wires are safely out of the puppy's way.

Inoculations
At approximately 12 weeks of age all puppies must be inoculated against Hepatitis, Leptospirosis, Distemper and Canine Parvovirus. Up until this time, the antibodies provided by their own dam have given them protection and would, in themselves, inhibit the vaccine from taking effect. These vaccinations are given in two injections administered two weeks apart. Not until your puppy has received its second dose is it safe to take it for walks in the street or to meet other dogs.

25

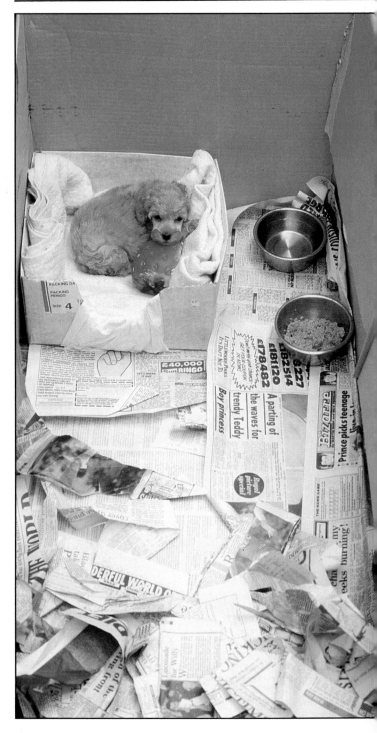

Left: *A temporary home-made cardboard pen for the puppy — make sure the sides are firm.*

Above: *The substitute litter — when in use, the bottle must be completely covered, the clock closed and also covered.*

The first night

A young puppy's first night in your home will be its first experience of being alone without the warmth and comfort of its litter brothers and sisters. Needless to say, it will not be an enjoyable experience for the puppy or its new owner. Feeling cold and lonely, it will undoubtedly start howling, and of course the longer it howls, the more cold and lonely the puppy will become. The problem arises on which course of action to take. Should you scold and leave alone in the hope that the puppy will tire itself out? Or should you pick the puppy up, soothe and take it to your own bed?

Both these solutions are really quite unsatisfactory. On no account go into the room to scold the puppy. What the puppy really wants is your company, so this will not worry the dog at all. Stand outside the door and scold in a firm voice. If you give in you will have nights of trouble. Unless you are prepared for the puppy to sleep in your bedroom for all time, do not let it sleep with you 'just this once'.

The substitute litter

By far the best idea in preventing this problem is to provide a comfortable bed with substitutes for the litter mates that the puppy will be missing. See if you can purchase an old-fashioned stone hot water bottle (not rubber, as the puppy may chew it). Wrap it securely in a blanket and place it in the puppy's sleeping box to provide extra warmth. The addition of a softly-ticking, closed travelling clock will provide a substitute for the heart-beats of the missing litter mates, and a child's soft toy will be a further consolation.

It is advisable to surround the bed with a fine wire mesh similar to a child's play pen. These puppy pens are available at most pet stores or can easily be made at home. Alternatively, you can make a pen out of large, cardboard boxes. The pen should be high enough to prevent the puppy climbing out, and should also be big enough to enable you to leave plenty of newspaper outside the box, where the puppy can relieve itself on waking. Puppies rarely, if ever, soil their beds.

After two or three nights, the puppy will learn when it is bed-time and will quickly accept the bed and pen as its own domain. Remember that a young puppy, like a small child, requires plenty of sleep during the day as well as night-time.

FEEDING

All puppies and growing dogs need more food per day than the adult dog; four meals a day are necessary when young. When fully mature, one or at the most two meals a day are then sufficient. The quantities depend on the size of the dog and the amount of energy it expends in exercise (see page 40 for a guide to quantities of food required by the adult dog). A Standard Poodle requires much more than a Miniature or a Toy. The correct amount of food for each variety of Poodle should be given to you by the breeder who will know from experience the best times of the day to feed the puppy and how much food is required for maximum growth and healthiness.

All dogs require a range of different types of food in order to promote a healthy and sound body:

Protein
This is essential. Obtainable in all dairy foods, meat, fish, poultry, rabbit, cereal and soya, all of which will promote a good body.

Fat, starch, sugar
Needed to provide energy, calcium and phosphorus. Contained in dairy foods.

Liver, kidney, wholemeal bread
To provide iron.

Vitamins
Vitamins are as important to dogs as ourselves. The chart opposite gives the source of these vitamins in natural foods.

It is important to note that ready-made adult and puppy foods from reputable manufacturers, if fed as

directed, do not need any vitamin or mineral supplement. At best they do no good; at worst they cause harm.

Most of the vitamins detailed in the chart can, of course, be obtained in powder or tablet form. I personally prefer natural sources

Above: *The puppy should be fed in a quiet atmosphere, with a large, clean plastic mat placed under the food and water bowls.*

and keep this chart in my kitchen for constant reference.

Vitamin Sources

Vit A: Egg, milk, butter, animal fats and cod liver oil — necessary for resistance to disease and growth.

Vit B: Wholemeal bread, eggs, vegetables and yeast — required regularly for the nervous system, energy and a good appetite.

Vit C: Fresh fruit, ie orange juice, and vegetables which purify the blood. Dogs synthesize their own Vitamin C, so it is not essential.

Vit D: Liver and cod liver oil — for good bones.

Vit E: Oats, wheat germ, olive oil and lettuce — for fertility.

As mentioned before, do, on purchasing your puppy, be sure to ask the breeder for a diet sheet. Individual Poodles vary in their dietary daily needs, and the breeder will know exactly how much food your puppy requires in the early months to ensure that it grows into a healthy and happy adult.

Feed at the same time every day. Do not at any time give your puppy any cooked bones, as these will splinter and could cause damage to the dog. All bones should be removed from rabbit, fish and chicken for the same reason. A raw beef bone is safe, greatly appreciated and will prevent the puppy chewing other things about the house. All food should be served at a reasonable temperature, never too hot nor frozen, and served in a quiet atmosphere. Too much noise can prevent a puppy from eating. Do not leave food in the bowl. If not eaten within ten minutes, remove until the next meal. Dogs do not chew, so it is quite natural for them to bolt their food very quickly. Dogs and puppies should always rest after a meal.

Canned foods

As a breeder, I recommend to owners acquiring a pet for the first time that they start their puppy's meals with a reputable canned puppy food — fed as a complete diet, or with plain biscuit meal or wholemeal toast. When fed according to instructions on the can, the puppy will rarely, in my experience, suffer from an upset stomach, which can occur while it is settling in at its new home.

Quantities

The best way of knowing just how much food your puppy requires is to watch it eating. If the puppy empties its dish quickly and seems to be looking for more, slightly increase the amount. It will take puppies no more than a few minutes to finish their food.

A suggested diet for a puppy

From two to four months. Give meals at regular times according to the daily routine of the household.

Breakfast: Any cereal with a little warm milk (not All Bran) with a little honey or glucose added, or a reputable canned puppy food with mixer.
or
Scrambled egg with a little well-toasted wholemeal bread.

Mid-day: Any of the following: raw beef, cooked beef, lamb, rabbit or a slice from any cooked joint of meat, all cut up into small pieces; a reputable canned puppy food, with or without puppy meal; cooked chicken (no bones); white fish (no bones) plus a little biscuit, wholemeal bread or puppy meal or grated carrot. Soya is also a good source of protein.

Tea-time: A digestive biscuit or toasted wholemeal bread
or
A drink of orange juice.

Supper: Same as Mid-day.

Cod liver oil given daily, quantities according to instructions on the bottle. Milk is not a natural food for dogs, it can cause loose bowel movement. Before bed-time, offer something similar to tea-time, but do not give too much liquid otherwise you will undoubtedly find a puddle in the morning.

Fresh clean water must **always** be available.

TRAINING

House training/breaking

One of the most important things to understand and to always remember is that young puppies have very little control, but if raised under good, clean conditions most have a natural instinct to be clean. Very rarely, even from three weeks of age, will a puppy soil its bed if it is possible to find another spot. A puppy will soon decide where it wishes to relieve itself. It is therefore up to you to make sure it chooses the right spot. The 'right spot' to start with can be newspaper put down in the same place, in any room where the puppy is running free. You soon learn by the puppy's behaviour the signs which are always the same. When the puppy wants to relieve itself, it will firstly sniff the floor circling around to find the right spot. When you see the puppy doing this, pick it up and take it outside. Stay with the puppy until it has done what is expected, then praise lavishly. If you leave, it will just follow you; a few minutes spent with the puppy at this stage will achieve far more.

Puppies should be taken outisde immediately after they wake and after every meal before resting.

However, puppies should not be taken outside in wet weather. In this case put the puppy on the newspaper, making sure it stays there until relieved. Again, remember to give plenty of praise.

If from an early age the puppy is trained to use newspaper, this training will be of great use to owners living in flats when it is not always possible, due to bad weather, to go for the necessary early and late walks. If you always place the newspaper in the same place, the puppy will soon understand its use.

The occasional mistake will occur; paper, grass and carpet will seem very similar to a puppy. To avoid any risk of stains on the carpet, spray neat fizzy soda water on the soiled spot, leave a few seconds then soak up with tissue or pieces of kitchen towel.

In addition to training a dog to be clean at home, it is equally important that it is trained to behave properly in public places. It is unlawful for a dog to foul the pavements or public footpaths, so it

Below: *This is a typical pose of a puppy circling with its nose down sniffing the paper prior to relieving itself.*

must be taught to use the gutter, grass or rough ground. Always carry a plastic bag or a 'poop-scoop' to remove any accidents immediately. You can be fined for failure to do so.

Jumping up

All Poodles need affection, quite often shown by jumping up to their owners and visitors. This is not always appreciated, as dirty paws can be unwelcome to even the greatest dog lover. This habit can be quickly stopped once the puppy realises it can be praised and patted with all feet on the ground. As soon as the puppy jumps up, hold it down on the ground with the command 'down'. When the puppy is still, praise and fondle it. However, do always remember to give the dog a greeting and a pat when it is well behaved.

Always remember in all training to be patient, affectionate and understanding. Give your puppy plenty of time and it will learn and understand all that is required. Also, do spend some time just playing for fun; a few games will be enjoyed by both you and the puppy.

Puppy training

The owner's early behaviour towards and understanding of a puppy will establish its health and character as an adult dog. For the first few days while it is assimilating so many new experiences, the puppy will spend most of its time exploring the new surroundings, eating, and sleeping. Nevertheless, the puppy will need to learn several things quite quickly, bearing in mind that it will have very little idea, if any, of what is expected.

First of all, the puppy needs to know its name. Call the puppy, and when it comes to you, praise and reward it with a titbit. Within a very short time, the puppy will recognise its name immediately, and you will have established the first step towards obedience.

On no account must you call the puppy's name for any unpleasant reason. It is vital for the dog's protection and your peace of mind that when it is called by name and comes to you, the word is associated with only pleasurable experiences.

The word 'no' must be used in a firm voice whenever the puppy does anything wrong. Make your tone of voice very stern. Dogs understand the **tone** of the human voice, not the words; you must use tone to differentiate between praising and blaming.

Left: *It is important to teach your puppy to lie down and stay down. Slide the sitting dog's front feet forward so it is lying down, at the same time saying 'down' firmly. Then back off a few paces and wait for a short time before returning to praise.*

Above: *Teach your puppy to sit and stay in the same way. Make the dog sit by pressing down the hindquarters while saying 'sit', back away and wait before praising and giving a titbit.*

Right: *These two 'poop-scoops' are a boon on any occasion, enabling dog owners to remove excrement quickly, hygienically and as pleasantly as possible from pathways or pavements.*

Lead training

Once a puppy is clean and regular in its habits and has learnt its name, the next essential stage is training the puppy to walk with a collar and lead. To achieve this, use the soft collar and lead purchased for use in the garden. Let the puppy get used to the collar first by keeping it on during the day while the dog runs loose around the garden. When the collar no longer bothers the puppy, attach the lead and once again let the dog wander on its own. But always keep a watch on the puppy in case the lead gets caught up on an obstacle, thereby causing distress or injury to the dog. After a few minutes running free, pick up the end of the lead and go where the puppy chooses. As soon as the puppy realises it is no longer free, it

Ready for its first lesson in the garden, the light-weight collar and lead are ideal for this purpose. Let the puppy wander on its own wearing the collar and lead, before picking up the lead. The puppy will begin to buck and struggle as soon as it realises it is no longer free. But with plenty of patience and words of encouragement, plus rewarding praise and titbits for added inducement, the puppy will gradually improve until it is walking to heel quite naturally. The tone of your voice must always convey strongly either your approval or displeasure. Finally, at the end of the lesson — which should be no longer than five minutes per day with a young puppy to be effective — do praise and pet your dog lavishly.

will buck and struggle. At this point, stand quite still. Eventually the puppy will stop, and when it does, very gently pull the lead towards you calling its name. When the puppy comes, which it will do eventually, reward it with much praise and a titbit. When the puppy ceases to struggle and comes to you quickly after the lead is pulled, walk slowly away from the dog giving the lead a gentle tug and calling its name. If it sits down just wait, do not pull. Wait until the puppy stands and try again. Five minutes training a day is ample. Lessons of short duration given often are by far the most effective.

Once the puppy is fully trained on its soft collar and lead, these can be discarded and it will accept the strong collar and lead with ease.

HOME HEALTH CARE

A puppy requires a little special attention at least once a day to its eyes, ears, teeth, feet and coat.

Eyes
The eye rims should be bathed by using cotton wool dipped in cool water or a mild solution of Boracic, dissolved in cool water, to clear any mucus from the corners.

Ears
Ears should be examined to make sure they are clean and sweet smelling. Any discharge or odour will require veterinary attention.

Teeth
It is advisable to get your puppy used to having its teeth cleaned at a young age at least once a week using a canine toothpaste. This is most important in the Toys. If your Poodle will not accept tooth brushing, try an application of hydrogen peroxide mouthwash or baking salt dissolved in water using a soft rag wrapped around the finger. Sadly, your best efforts may not be tolerated and regular scaling and polishing under anesthesia by your veterinarian will be the only effective way of maintaining the teeth.

Hard-baked biscuits, large chunks of fibrous meat, raw beef bones and chew bones all help with oral hygiene.

At the time you choose your puppy, it will still have its baby or 'milk' teeth, to be replaced by permanent teeth at six to seven months of age or older. Before the latter erupt, small amounts of fluoride should be given — similar to a human baby's dose. If in doubt, seek specialist veterinary advice.

Coat
Brush the coat daily with a soft bristle brush. As the puppy matures, a stiffer brush will be necessary. Brush right down to the skin, then comb the coat right through, not forgetting the ear fringes and tail.

Feet
Check the pads for any foreign bodies or cuts. Keep the nails clipped short, otherwise they will grow too long and could easily get torn off. Nails are difficult to cut as it is important not to cut the *quick*.

Below: *The Poodle's feet should have short, well-cut nails. The darker* quick *can be clearly seen in this puppy's white nail.*

Above: *Bathe the puppy's eyes morning and evening, using a different piece of cotton wool for each eye to cleanse.*

The latter is easy to see in young puppies and some adults if the nails are white, but with black nails great care is needed. Clip, with nail clippers, a little at a time (see page 44). If in doubt, a quick visit to a veterinarian is advisable.

Parasites
The Poodle puppy is prone to infection by a variety of parasites, as detailed below. See also the section on parasites in Chapter 3.

Roundworms Most puppies have these worms *(toxocara canis);* they are born with the larvae in their bodies, which develop into adult worms by the time the puppy is two weeks of age. The adult worm can be up to 5in (13cm) long and produces microscopic eggs which can exist in the ground or in your home for a very long time. They are a health hazard, particularly to young children in warm, damp conditions.

As mentioned before, you should make a note of the dates when the puppy was wormed when you collect it from the breeder. Ideally, it will have been wormed at two and a half to three weeks of age, and subsqently at two-week intervals. The worming treatment should continue every two weeks until the puppy reaches three months of age, then again at six months of age. Visit your veterinarian to discuss the worming programme and to obtain the necessary treatment — usually in tablet form. Proprietary preparations are only about 60% effective.

Ear mites These parasites are the commonest cause of ear disease in the Poodle. The mites live on skin debris on the surface of the ear canal. They can cause intense irritation and the production of reddish-brown crusts. The infection is highly contagious and is especially prevalent in young animals. Mineral oils combined with an insecticide are effective as long as the treatment is maintained for a four-week period. The dog's environment should be treated as thoroughly as the dog itself.

Cheyletiella mites (walking dandruff) This is a parasite that can cause unpleasant irritation to the owner as well as the pet host. The mites live only on the host and consquently are easier to deal with. The mites and eggs can be seen with a magnifying lens, but the appearance of fine dandruff on the coat gives a clue to their presence. Most insecticides are effective but should be applied three times at weekly intervals.

Scabies (sarcoptic mange) This mite produces an intensely itchy, non-seasonal, transmissible infection. The mites burrow in the superficial layers of the skin, and can live on human beings for at least six days. The infection is highly contagious and young animals are more susceptible.

As the mite lives most of its life below the surface of the skin, it can be difficult to diagnose, even by repeated skin scrapings examined microscopically. Your veterinarian may make a diagnosis purely on the appearance of the patient. Although insecticides are effective, hair will need to be clipped away and other medications used to relieve irritation and remove skin scale. Again, the dog's environment should be treated with an insecticide at the same time.

Chapter Three

THE ADULT POODLE

Feeding
Exercise
Home health care
Travelling
Old age

FEEDING

The age of maturity, when you can start the change from puppy meals to adult food, differs according to the variety of Poodle. A Toy Poodle is mature at approximately seven months, a Miniature Poodle at about nine to ten months, while the Standard poodle is not considered fully grown until approximately 20 months of age.

The adult Poodle can be fed once a day. This can be at any time convenient to the family, morning or evening. The golden rule is: you must always feed at the same time every day. Clean, fresh water **must** be available at all times.

Quantities

In recommending the quantity of food to be fed daily to your adult Poodle, several factors must be considered. If your Poodle is a pet given limited exercise, it will not require as much food as the country dog running free all day. A busy stud dog requires extra food, as does a brood bitch. But as a rough guide the usual requirements are considered to be ½oz (14g) of food for 1lb (454g) of body weight plus biscuit or cereal per day. But all Poodles, be they Standards, Miniatures or Toys, vary in their dietary requirements, so to give exact amounts is quite useless. Like people, some Poodles eat a lot and keep thin, whilst others get fat with very little food. It is up to the owner to learn to gauge the amount suitable for his or her own dog.

Canned foods

Great advances have been made recently in the quality of canned dog foods. For convenience and time-saving, the many well-established manufacturers of canned food can be relied on to provide nutritious and substantial meals for all sizes of Poodles fed as a complete diet.

Dried foods

Meal or dried foods are also available. Once again, the well-

Above: *A Standard Poodle living in the country with a young and energetic owner will need more food than a city dog.*

established brands are considered to be nutritious and satisfying for health and growth. Some are fed dry whilst others need to be served moist. Always feed according to the manufacturer's instructions printed on all packets.

Variety	Body weight	Food per day
Standard	60lb (27kg)	1-1½lb (453-680g) + meal/biscuit
Miniature	14-18lb (6.3-8kg)	6-8oz (170-227g) + meal/biscuit
Toy	6-12lb (3-5kg)	4-6oz (113-170g) + meal/biscuit

EXERCISE

In discussing the question of how much exercise is necessary for each variety of Poodle, it is impossible to give a general ruling as so many factors must be taken into consideration: the size and age of the Poodle, where you live, whether the Poodle lives alone or shares its life with another dog. Two Toy or Miniature Poodles living together in a home with a fairly large garden, if given their freedom, will run and play together until they tire out naturally. A Standard Poodle living in restricted circumstances is a very frustrated animal. These dogs do require much more exercise than the smaller varieties. Even in a relatively large garden, the Standard will require at least 1½-2 hours of exercise a day. This can take the form of very long walks or, preferably, being allowed to run free but under supervision in the country or large open spaces. Miniatures require between ½-1 hour per day, Toys approximately

½ hour. Beware of over-exercising the very small Toy Poodle.

While on the question of exercise, remember that all dogs away from their home must wear a collar with their owner's name and address. No dog should be allowed out on its own. If it should cause any accident or damage in any way, you, as the dog's owner, would be liable. When out in public places with your dog, it should be under your control. Never let it foul anywhere people might walk or where children may play. Use the gutter in an emergency and carry a plastic bag to remove any excrement immediately.

Below: *Ch Montravia Tommy Gun, the top-winning show Poodle of all times, still enjoys a romp with his owner, Marita Gibbs.*

HOME HEALTH CARE

A well reared, fed and exercised Poodle should require little care when adult, but a daily routine inspection of eyes, ears, anal glands, teeth, nails and pads, combined with regular grooming (see Chapter Four), will enable you to notice any problems at an early stage that may require veterinary attention.

Eyes
Poodles frequently have runny eyes, more obviously seen on Whites and Apricots but often present in all varieties. This problem can be difficult and frustrating for even a veterinarian to sort out, but regular cleaning with proprietary preparations will improve the eyes' appearance and reduce local skin problems.

If the eyes are inflamed or discharging pus, look for foreign bodies such as grass seeds, then bathe with cotton wool and cool water. If the Poodle appears to be in pain from the examination or bathing, seek immediate veterinary attention.

Ears
These should always be pink and clean, without any unpleasant odour. Use a cotton wool bud dipped in almond or olive oil to clean inside the ear, but on no account probe deep into the ear recess. If this recess looks dirty and has an unpleasant odour, a visit to a veterinarian is necessary.

Hair should be plucked from ears between finger and thumb about every six weeks. Neglected ears become inflamed and the lining painful and thickened. Surgery may then be the only treatment. Sometimes a Poodle may really resent the plucking, in which case be extra vigilant in your checks for smell and discharge.

Anal glands
These are located each side of the anus and should be regularly checked as, unless kept clear, they can become blocked often causing an abscess to form. If you see any signs of your Poodle pulling itself along the ground while sitting down, or running around after its tail, it is wise to examine these glands. Mild cases are quite easy, if somewhat unpleasant, to deal with. As these glands are situated close to the anal passage, with pressure from your thumb and finger exerted each side of the anus, they will quickly empty. It is a good idea to ask your veterinarian or the breeder to show you this method, which will enable you to prevent any further trouble in the future.

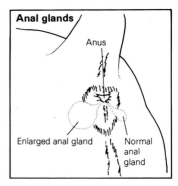

Above: *The dog's anal glands lie just under the skin slightly below and on each side of the anus. They normally empty themselves when a motion is passed. They cannot be felt when empty but are grapedsized when full.*

Teeth
Always make sure your Poodle's teeth are in good condition by regular brushing at least once a week using a canine toothpaste.

Soft and sloppy food will cause tartar to form very quickly. This can be removed with a dental scaler, but care must be taken to make sure the scaler is inserted between the gum and the tartar, when, with experience, the tartar will chip off with ease. However, as most Poodles resent this treatment, a quick visit to a veterinarian will save you what could be a difficult task.

A careful watch should be kept

Teeth of the adult dog

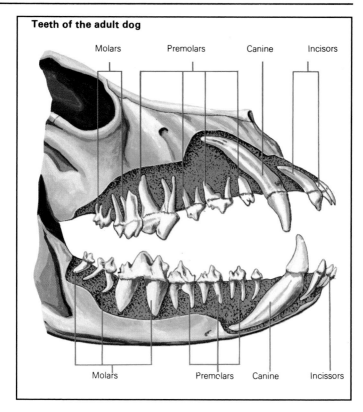

Molars   Premolars   Canine   Incisors

Molars   Premolars   Canine   Incissors

on the state of the teeth. Any sign of decay or redness of the gums will need expert attention. Bad teeth, especially in the older dog, are often the cause of bad health.

Retention of baby teeth can cause long-term problems with the

Below: *Carefully pluck the hair from your Poodle's ears once every six weeks. This will prevent the ears becoming inflamed, and a thickening of the lining, causing your pet pain. In severe cases of neglect, surgery may be required.*

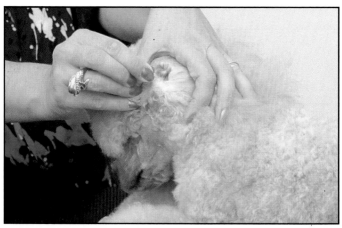

permanent teeth. As a general guide, when all the permanent teeth have erupted — from six to seven months of age — the baby teeth should all have fallen out. If there are any baby teeth left at this stage, contact your veterinarian who will arrange for them to be removed under general anesthetic. A full complement of permanent teeth amounts to 42. In the upper jaw, there should be six incisors, and two canines, one on each side of the incisors. Behind each canine are four premolars on each side, making 20 in all. In the lower jaw the distribution is identical except for the molars, of which there are three on each side making 22 teeth in all.

Your veterinarian will advise you about problems of malocclusion, ie teeth in the wrong position when the jaws are brought together, and over or undershot jaws (see illustrations in Chapter Seven).

Nails
With well-constructed Poodle feet and plenty of exercise on hard surfaces, the nails will rarely require cutting. Unfortunately, many

Below: *Three types of nail clippers — the guillotine type (centre) is perhaps the easiest to use. A dab of permanganate will stop any bleeding. Use a file to smooth rough edges.*

Poodles have loose feet with slightly splayed pads and nails which require cutting fairly often, as they grow very quickly. The *quick* descends down the nail, making it difficult to cut without causing pain. Cut the nails using strong nail clippers or a special guillotine cutter for dogs' nails. If the nail is light in colour, it is usually possible to see and remove the dead section, taking care not to cut into the bloodline. Black nails are much more difficult, so cut a little at a time. If you do cause the nail to bleed, a dab of permanganate of potash or a styptic pencil will stop the bleeding quite quickly. After cutting the nails, file them smooth with a special nail file for dogs, usually available from pet stores selling grooming equipment.

Parasites
The adult Poodle can be troubled by a range of internal and external parasites, in addition to those detailed in Chapter Two.

Roundworms Adult Poodles should be treated with medication prescribed by your veterinarian once every six months throughout their lives.

Tapeworms Seek veterinary advice when you suspect tapeworms. They are not directly a health hazard to the family (with

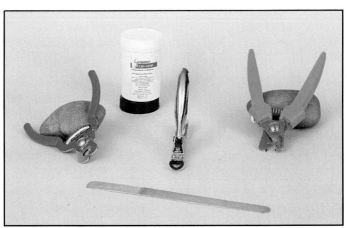

one rare exception — see below), but proprietary remedies are rarely effective. The worm needs a secondary host, usually a rodent or flea, to complete its lifecycle. A sign of infection is the appearance of segments of the worm crawling around the dog's anus; they resemble cucumber seeds or grains of rice.

In areas where hydatid disease is present, regular tapeworm doses should be administered. This tapeworm of dogs is contracted from sheep or deer, and the eggs can infect people.

There are few signs of illness associated with tapeworms in dogs, except in heavy infestation when diarrhoea and weight loss occur.

Heartworms These are parasitic worms that are found in dogs' hearts. Dogs are the only mammals commonly affected, and the worm is transmitted by a mosquito. It is found in Africa, Asia and in large areas of the US, particularly the East Coast. In areas where the disease is endemic, daily preventative treatment is essential during the mosquito season. Seek local veterinary advice, and have yearly blood tests to confirm freedom from the infection.

Fleas These are very common, and they are not particular about where they live or who they bite. They have increased with the advent of central heating and fitted carpets. Fleas do not need to live on you or your pet; they just need a warm-blooded body to feed off when they are hungry. Because they are small and active, you may not actually see them. But you can spot where they have been by noticing the dark brown droppings when you are grooming.

Flea control is an important part of pet care. They can cause skin problems if your pet is allergic to their bite, and they can also cause you to have irritating red spots. Insecticides are now available which actually inhibit flea reproduction - a great advance. It is vital to treat your dog and its

environment at the same time. When using insecticides, follow the manufacturer's instructions carefully. These products must kill the fleas but not the host.

Demodectic mange This is a curious parasite which can exist in large numbers of dogs without causing symptoms. When it does, treatment can be lengthy and difficult. Most animals can now be cured, although because the illness may represent an immune failure, dogs having had the disease should not be bred from, unless the condition was only transient. Seek expert veterinary advice.

Lice (prediculosis) Lice are spread by direct contact or by contaminated brushes and combs. They accumulate under mats of hair around the ears, neck and body openings causing intense irritation. Since the insects are only $1/10$in (3mm) long, they are difficult to see in Poodle hair. If you suspect infestation, bathe your dog using an insecticidal shampoo (see Chapter Four, pages 60-61 on bathing) three times at weekly intervals and clip matted hair away (see pages 62-67 on clipping). Lice live and breed entirely on the dog, so it is not vital to treat the dog's environment as well.

Ticks Dogs can pick up ticks by running through grass, woods or sandy beaches. These blood-sucking insects bury their barbed mouths firmly into the dog's skin, causing irritation and often resulting in secondary skin infections. To remove adult ticks, soak them with ether, surgical spirit or tick spray. This will loosen the head and mouthparts to enable the removal of the whole insect with tweezers. The dog can be regularly bathed in a tick dip to prevent infestation, especially if it is in contact with sheep. The dog's environment should be vigorously disinfected as in some countries ticks transmit serious diseases such as anaplasmosis and babesiosis, and can cause tick paralysis.

TRAVELLING

One of the worst aspects of travelling with dogs is the fact that so many of them suffer from car sickness. I have discovered from experience that if you get puppies used to the car between seven and nine weeks of age, they very rarely suffer from car sickness.

Boxes and Cages

When they mature, I have found that Poodles prone to travel sickness are less likely to suffer if they are boxed, with good ventilation and forward vision only. The flashing by of trees, sky, signs or pylons overhead seems to disturb them, often causing nervousness and sickness.

It is much safer for the Miniature and Toy Poodles to travel in covered cages or boxes. I often hear pet owners say that they consider it cruel to put dogs in these boxes. How wrong they are! If the box or cage is made comfortable with a warm blanket in winter and a cool layer of cotton in the summer, any small dog will come to regard its box as its own special property. With the door of the box or cage left open at home, the dog will retire voluntarily to this refuge whenever sleepy or needing a rest. Select a cage or box of the right size for your Poodle from a pet store or supplier; it must be large enough for the dog to stand up and turn around. Always make sure the fastenings are secure.

On a long car journey, safe in their familiar boxes, the Toys and Miniatures will be both secure and relaxed. The driver will also be secure in the knowledge that there is no fear of a sprightly Poodle jumping on him or her, or, if it is suddenly necessary to brake quickly, that no harm will come to the dog.

Right: Two safe travelling boxes, both light and easy to carry. The open cage will require a cover if used in winter.

Above: This cage is too small for the Poodle inside — the dog would have difficulty in standing up or turning round in the cage.

Right: Cages are also invaluable for transporting Miniature and Toy Poodles to dog shows. Unlike the cage above, this Toy has plenty of room to lie down and rest.

Dog guards

Standard Poodles; due to their size, are rarely boxed. If you are planning to take your Poodle in the car, install a dog guard. This restricts the dog to the rear of the car, where it can lie in comfort and remain safe and protected.

The parked car

One of the most alarming and distressing failures of many owners is their habit of occasionally leaving their dogs in parked cars. Weather conditions can change rapidly, from cloud and rain to bright sunshine in only a few minutes. Even if you park the car in a cool, shady position, in time the sun will move round. Such changes will raise the heat in the car interior alarmingly.

A small opening in a window is quite useless once the sun shines. If the windows are opened sufficiently for plenty of air to circulate, the dog will quickly escape. The interior of a car can heat to a temperature of 120°F (49°C) and over. In such heat, a dog will sink into a coma and die within 15 minutes or sooner. **Never leave your Poodle in a parked car.**

Above: *Although the car window is open, if the car was left in the sun even for a short time, this Poodle could become a very distressed animal.*

OLD AGE IN THE POODLE

As your Poodle gets older you will notice a number of changes in its behaviour and appearance. The dog will have far less stamina and require only the minimum of exercise. Its eyes can fail and its hearing become impaired. The skin becomes loose on the body, with white hairs appearing firstly on the muzzle of all the Poodle colours except the White. The pigment on the nose will also fade with age and often the Poodle will start to put on weight.

There are many ways of keeping the old dog happy. Established routines of feeding and exercise should be continued with a reduction in food as the amount of exercise lessens. Make sure the dog has a warm, comfortable bed. Do not let it get wet or cold, and keep it out of draughts.

Above: *This is a lovely study of a Poodle in its advanced years, still handsome despite the addition of a number of white hairs on the muzzle and in the ear feathering.*

Below: *Here, two elderly Poodles are seen enjoying the warmth and comfort of their home, which is the right of all dogs when they reach their advanced years.*

Old age in dogs is often accompanied by various illnesses, both minor and severe. Nearly all can be treated by modern drugs, but the time will come when you may have to decide when its life must end. So many owners prolong the so called 'life' of their pets for selfish reasons; a point is reached when the owner is prolonging death not life. As a loving and responsible owner, the last kindness you can give your devoted friend and companion for many years is a quick and painless release from suffering and a life without 'living'.

Chapter Four

GROOMING AND CLIPPING

The Clips
Show clipping
Pet grooming and clipping

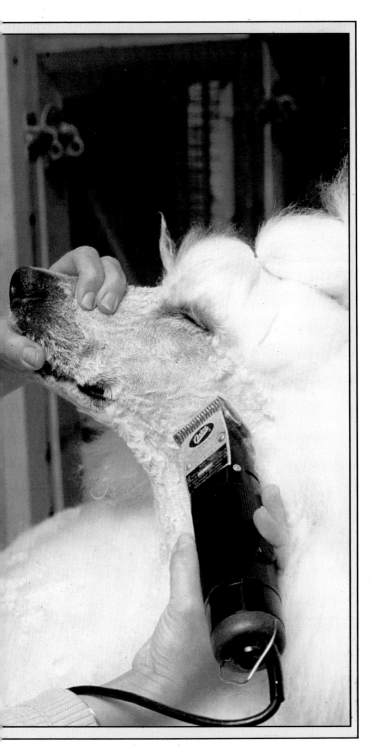

THE CLIPS

Poodles were considered in the past as water dogs, and were used for many centuries as gun dogs retrieving game shot down over rivers and lakes. They were therefore clipped with the mane left long to protect the heart and lungs, and their hindquarters, arms and legs shaved to facilitate swimming, bands of hair left to protect the wrists, knees and ankles. A 'pom-pom' of hair was left on the tail to act as a rudder. The final touch was a brightly-coloured ribbon on the 'top-knot', not only to prevent hair falling over the Poodle's eyes, but for the owners to recognise their own dogs at a distance. So originated the English Saddle or Lion Clip, a tradition which, like so many others, has lasted to the present day.

Modern clips

Over the years many fancy clipping styles have come and gone. The traditional Lion Clip, Continental Clip, Puppy Clip, and Lamb Clip are the four main styles of clipping today. The Puppy, Lion and Continental Clips are mostly reserved for the show ring. The Sporting Clip, a slightly modified form of the Lamb Clip, is acceptable when showing a Poodle in the Stud Dog and Brood Bitch classes in the US. The Lamb Clip has become the most acceptable to pet owners. The popularity of the Miniature and Toy Poodles as pets in the the late 1950s and early 1960s was mainly due to the introduction of the Lamb Clip. It enabled Poodle owners to keep their dogs well-groomed, neat and tidy, while looking attractive and stylish. The Lamb Clip is easily accomplished and very easy to maintain, and can, if allowed to grow, be converted into any variety of show clip.

For the Lamb Clip, the hair on the Poodle's face, feet and part of the tail is clipped closely and cleanly. The hair on the neck and body is left longer, to about 1in (2.5cm) in length, while the legs are scissored, rather than clipped, to roughly 2in (5cm), in length. The hair on the head and tail is shaped to make a 'pom-pom'; with the ears left long but the fringes tidied.

Below: *It is easy to understand how this attractive Lamb Trim helped popularize the breed in the 1960s; a lovely example.*

Above: *This beautiful White Standard highlights the elegance of the Continental Lion Clip as exhibited today.*

Below: *Another pet clip which is becoming increasingly popular both in the UK and in the US, called the Teddy Bear Trim.*

Right: *This beautiful, present-day White Miniature Champion looks both balanced and elegant. Note the perfect scissoring with well-shaped bracelets, pom-pom and mane. The head is lovely with the dark almond eye giving the Poodle its typical expression.*

Below: *This Standard Poodle, Ch Orchard Whiteboy born circa 1904 painted by F T Daws, illustrates how much presentation has changed. This dog lacks balance and elegance; the heavy, unshaped mane makes him look quite neckless.*

Show clipping

The Puppy Clip, permissible in the show ring until the Poodle is one year old, requires the face, feet and base of the tail to be clipped clean. The tail hair is shaped to a round 'pom-pom' with scissors, and the hair on the head, body and legs is combed out and slightly scissored to give a clean, natural outline. The ear fringes are left long and rounded neatly.

The present day excellence of presentation in all three sizes of Poodles in the show rings of Europe is, in my opinion, due in no small way to the American exhibitors who, over the years, have excelled in the grooming and scissoring of

many breeds, by no means least the Poodle. During 1966, Mrs Susan Fraser sent her Standard Poodle, the American/Canadian bred Eng Am & Can Ch Bibelots Tall Dark and Handsome, over to the UK for exhibition with the hope of gaining the title of English Champion. This the Poodle did with ease, winning Dog of the Year 1966 and Reserve Best in Show at Crufts 1967. This was the first opportunity that UK exhibitors had had to see a Poodle with the American presentation of the English Saddle Clip. The impact was instantaneous, and from that time the presentation has continually improved, which becomes obvious in comparison of

the presentation of Standards in the late 1950s with the superb presentation of the Supreme Champion at Crufts 1985, Ch Montravia Tommy Gun.

The English Saddle Clip of today is vastly different to that of the 1930s when the Clip consisted of profuse curly hair. The mane became longer and longer in order to balance the length of the 'saddle', with the 'puffs' and 'bracelets' being enlarged and lowered in an effort to counteract any top-heaviness, all resulting, in my opinion, in an overcoated, neckless dog with little elegance or balance.

The Continental Clip, out of favour for so many years has, during the past two decades, become more and more popular. With its clean and precise lines, it presents the elegant Poodle to perfection.

The two styles of clipping, compulsory for exhibition, are quite similar. The English Saddle leaves the hindquarters or 'saddle' closely trimmed, resembling the curl of a Persian lamb or, if combed out, a plush finish, with two 'bracelets' on each leg. With the Continental Clip, the hindquarters are clipped bare with a pom-pom over each hip (often referred to as 'kidney patches') and one pom-pom on each leg.

PET GROOMING & CLIPPING

I would like to bring to your notice a few points which, in my opinion, are important before any owner attempts to clip and groom his or her own Poodle.

Firstly, written instructions can help but cannot entirely teach you the correct and safe use of both clippers and scissors. For this I strongly advise a course in Poodle trimming given by experts. These courses are often advertised in the weekly or monthly dog magazines or journals.

I have limited detailed grooming instructions to the pet Poodle, and the Lamb or Pet Clip. The elegant and attractive Lion Clip is very difficult to master. Many months and even years are required to acquire the level of perfection necessary to present the Poodle at its best in this Clip. No two dogs are alike; one might be improved by a short style while another can benefit from a longer looser style. Both under an expert groomer will be improved in outline and overall balance. So, in addition to a knowledge of clipping and scissoring techniques, the expert will know from experience exactly how to present each individual Poodle according to its particular physical attributes, ie its conformation.

Equipment
If as a pet owner you wish to bath, clip and groom your own Poodle, it is necessary to acquaint yourself with the type and use of the correct grooming equipment.

Below: *Steel combs of various types and sizes. Most useful are the ones with half medium and half fine teeth. The comb top centre has revolving teeth excellent for dematting.*

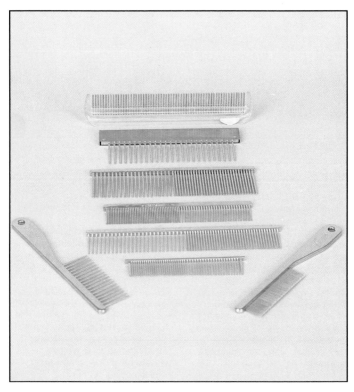

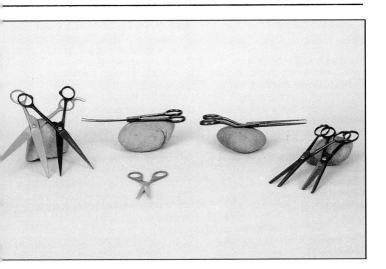

Above: *Various scissors, left to right — shears and 7in (18cm) for shaping mane, curved to do pom-poms and bracelets, two blunt-ended for safety, the small pair for between pads.*

Below: *Square slicker brushes for bracelets and short hair. Pin brushes with cushioned base for longer hair. Bristle and nylon or pure bristle best for mane, ear feathering and top-knot.*

A steel comb This should have rounded teeth at least 1½ in (4cm) long for the Standard Poodle. For Miniatures and Toys, you should use a steel comb with teeth between ¾ to 1in long (2-2.5cm). Most steel combs have half medium and half fine teeth.

Scissors Always buy scissors of good quality, preferably of stainless steel which will not rust. The length and type of scissors will depend on personal choice; a 7½ in (19cm) length is lighter to handle than shears of 8½ in (22cm). Scissors with blunt ends are useful for puppies and to scissor near the eyes.

Brushes A slicker brush with curved, dense pins should be used for the bracelets and short hair, a pin brush on a cushioned base for the longer hair, but a pure bristle brush is recommended for the mane and top-knot.

Clippers The size and type of clippers varies enormously, with different sized blades used for the different parts of the Poodle according to the length of hair required, ie much shorter on the face, feet and tail than on the body. The *Oster No 5* has interchangeable blades: No 15 for the short clip and No 5 for the body.

Hair dryers For the Miniature and Toy sizes, any hairdryer, providing it has a stand, is suitable. Both hands are needed to control the Poodle and to brush the hair dry at the same time. The Standard Poodle will require a much more powerful dryer such as used by professional groomers, with a good heat output.

Shampoo Special dog shampoos are available from pet stores, including insecticidal shampoos for the control of parasites. A tearless shampoo is very useful for puppies. There are numerous shampoos especially produced to enhance the coat; obviously a shampoo for White Poodles will not be suitable for the Blacks.

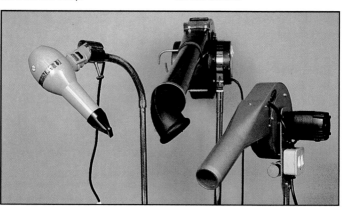

Above: *Three powerful hair dryers on stands, leaving both hands free to control and brush the Poodle while drying.*

Below: *There are many different types of clippers with blades of various sizes, depending on your requirements.*

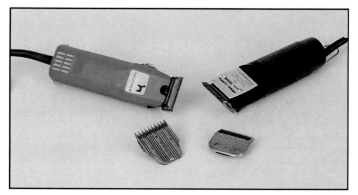

Combing and brushing

It is of the utmost importance
before you give your Poodle a bath
that the coat is thoroughly combed
and brushed right down to the skin.
This is best achieved by laying the
Poodle down on its side and
layering the hair. Comb first,
starting at the end of the hair, then
deeper until the comb is going
through the whole length of the
hair from the dog's skin to the ends
of the hair. Pay particular attention
to the areas under the forearms and
under the ears.

Above: *A professional groomer
shows how to hold a Poodle to
brush underneath the dog's body.
The best technique is to use brisk
strokes with the brush to lift the
hair rather than flatten it.*

Unless a Poodle coat is groomed
daily mats will occur, especially
during Spring and Autumn when
the coat changes. A matted coat
can become so bad that the only
solution is to shear it off
completely.

Bathing

Once your Poodle is free from mats bathing is quite easy. Place a piece of cotton wool in each ear, and wet the Poodle completely using a mixer spray and warm water. Shampoo well all over the body, legs and feet. Then, taking particular care not to allow the soap to get into the eyes, shampoo the head and ears. Rinse and shampoo again, then rinse until all soap is removed and the water runs clear. Squeeze as much water as possible out of the coat, remove cotton wool from the ears and wrap the dog in a warm towel. With your hair dryer, brush and blow dry a small area at a time, keeping the dryer on medium heat. When completely dry comb through from top to tail. Only then can you start trimming.

3 *Rinse the dog's coat until the water runs clear. Take care no water runs into the ears — these should be protected with cotton wool.*

4 *After rinsing remove as much surplus water from the Poodle's coat as possible. An absorbent sponge used as shown here will do the job most efficiently.*

1 *A rubber mat to stand on will prevent the dog slipping. Spray with warm water, shampoo body and legs first.*

2 *When shampooing the head, care must be taken. Soap in the eyes is painful. Hold the head as shown here.*

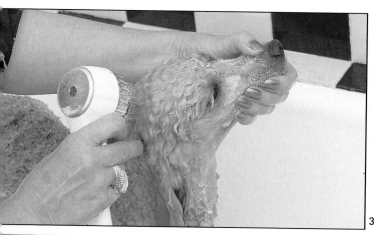

3

4

5 *Remove cotton wool from ears, wrap in a large warm towel to remove surplus water before starting to brush and dry.*

6 *This Poodle's coat looks clean and well-groomed. The final touches to the well-feathered ears will complete the attractive picture.*

5

6

The Lamb Clip

Step one With the Poodle sitting on a firm table, clip the feet upwards from the toes leaving 1in (2.5cm) of ankle exposed. To remove the hair between the pads, I prefer a small pair of blunt-ended scissors. Poodle feet are very sensitive, so be extra patient.

Step two Hold the clippers flat on the surface of the head and clip a straight line from in front of the ear to the outer corner of the eye, on both sides of the head.

Step three Starting 2-3in (5-8cm) down the throat just below the Adam's Apple, with the head held upwards remove hair in a triangle from the ears to the middle of the throat. Press jaws tightly together and remove hair from each side of the muzzle, starting below the eye. Finish by removing hair along the top of the muzzle to the nose.

Step four Comb ears, tidy up any uneven ends. Holding the head towards you, cut an inverted V between the top of the eyes. The point of the A should be in line with the top of the eyes.

Step five Shape the top-knot according to your preference either round or square in shape starting at the outer corner of the eye and working around over ear, cutting off all hair which falls over the clipped line between the eye and ear. Blend into clipped neck hair.

Step six Clip half the tail on the top side with the blade of the clippers towards the body, and underneath with the blade away from the body.

Step seven With a No 5 blade, clip from the base of the skull down the back, and along the back to the tail. Then clip down the shoulders and over the ribs and under the body to the last rib. Do not clip over the hips.

Step eight Comb, scissor and shape the legs. Blend into the hair on the body.

Your first attempt will probably exhaust you more than the Poodle. But no matter how disappointed you are with the finished result, next time it will be easier and you will do better, and eventually you will be proud of your achievement.

1 *When clipping the feet, hold the foot firmly with the fingers of your left hand placed underneath the pads for complete control.*

2 *By spreading the toes out with your free hand, it is possible with practice to remove the hair between the toes with the clipper edge.*

3

3 *When clipping from the ear to the outer corner of the eye in a straight line, hold the clipper flat on the surface. Be careful not to clip too close here.*

4 & 5 *Hold the jaws firmly together when clipping the muzzle, starting just below the eye. To clip hair on lips, stretch the loose skin with your free thumb for safety.*

4

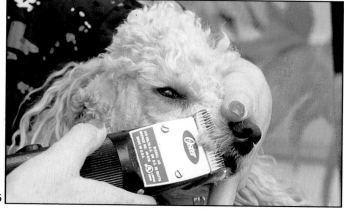

5

6

6 *When clipping the throat, hold the head upright; clip upwards for a close cut, downwards for a longer coat.*

7 *Comb out the hair of the top-knot and the feathering on the ears with care, making sure to remove any tangles or mats.*

7

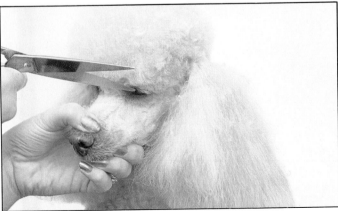

8

9

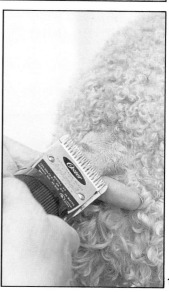

8 *Hold the head with your free hand and cut a line from the corner of the eye back over the top of the ear, and down back of neck.*

9 *Shape the top-knot by cutting from the right eye over the ear and round back of head. Repeat on left side. Comb and shape to leave the top-knot level with the eyes.*

10 *When docked correctly, the tail is divided into half pom-pom and half clipped. Clip top and sides of tail towards body, but underneath clip away from the body.*

11 *With the dog facing you, clip down the back of the dog, commencing at the base of the skull. Do not allow the blades of the clippers to get too hot because this can cause clipper rash.*

10

11

12 *Clip along the back of the Poodle to the root of the tail. Take care to keep the length of hair even by using a No 5 Oster blade.*

13 *When clipping the stomach, remove the side hair by lifting front leg or hold dog upright with your free hand to clip underneath.*

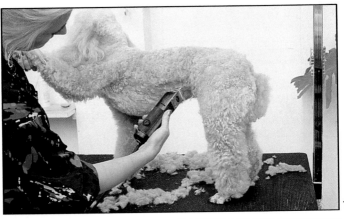

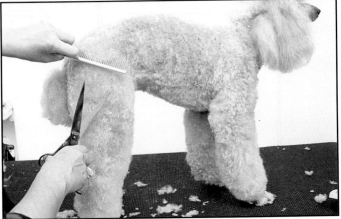

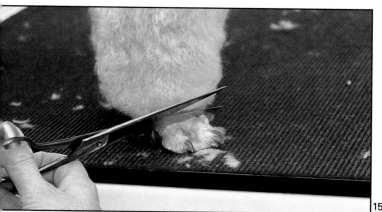

15

14 *After combing through the hair on the front and back legs, shape following the natural contours and blend with the body hair.*

15 *Comb hair down at the ankles and scissor the coat just above the pads making sure to remove all the untidy hair to give the legs a neat and finished look.*

16 *This shows the finished head. The top-knot is well-shaped and framed by lovely ear fringes. Two brightly-coloured hair bows have been tied to the ear feathering.*

17 *This Miniature Poodle can now rest after its full grooming session. This is the typical 'lamb' look, with a good evenness of coat and attractive head style.*

16

17

Chapter Five

VETERINARY CARE

Your first visit
Infections prevented by vaccination
Common ailments and diseases
Specific breed problems

YOUR FIRST VISIT

Choose your veterinarian carefully — remember you and the vet are your dog's best friends.

In reception, make sure you get a card with consultation times and details of emergency services. Most surgeries will have a 'pet pack' for new owners with much useful information. Take one home.

The main reason for this visit is to check for general health, and any sign of congenital or hereditary deformity.

The examination
Now for your puppy's first examination. The veterinarian will be having a good look at the puppy while listening to your account of feeding habits, behaviour and how it is settling into the family. You should have papers from the breeder with information on diet, worming and previous vaccinations. The veterinarian may ask for a stool sample to check for worms.

The temperature of the puppy will be taken, and ears, eyes, heart and joints checked. If the veterinarian suspects the presence

of a serious congenital or hereditary defect, it may be advisable to send the puppy back to the breeder, particularly if you have plans to show or breed from your dog. The most frequently spotted defects at this stage in Poodles are luxating patellae (slipping knee caps), entropion (turning in of the eyelids) and cryptorchidism (absence of one or both testicles in the scrotum). Distichiasis (extra hairs sprouting from the eyelid margin) and patent ductus arteriosus (a defect in the circulation) are two other conditions not infrequently spotted in Poodles at this first examination.

A health programme
Having passed the physical examination you must now discuss feeding and general management, and a worming and vaccination programme.

If it is your first experience with a pet, make sure you have a list of questions to cover all your queries.

Below: *It is important to visit a veterinarian with your new puppy for a thorough health check as soon as possible after purchase.*

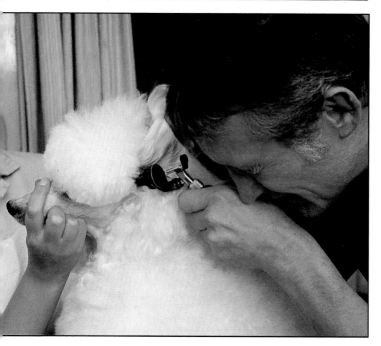

INFECTIONS PREVENTED BY VACCINATION

Above: *Here the veterinarian is checking deep into the Poodle's ears for any signs of infection using a special instrument called an auriscope.*

Rabies

This is a virus disease that is always fatal once symptoms show. It can be transmitted to man. Rabies is a disease of the central nervous system, and manifests itself in two forms, 'furious' and 'dumb'. 'Furious' rabies is comparatively easy to diagnose. The 'dumb' form, which is characterised by paralysis, is not spectacular and is difficult to diagnose, despite being more common than the furious form.

Wildlife act as reservoir for the disease: racoons and skunks in the US, vampire bats in South America, the mongoose in South Africa and the fox in Western and Eastern Europe.

Incubation can be between five days and ten months. Affected animals show a change in temperament, becoming highly restless and irritable. As the disease progresses there is weakness of the tail and legs, difficulty in swallowing, and drooping of the jaw and eyelids. The animal usually dies in a state of coma, following convulsive seizures in the furious form and paralysis in the dumb form.

Vaccination is now effective and is mandatory in some areas of the world, such as the USA. Booster vaccinations are yearly or biannually in some states.

Canine parvovirus (CPV)

A virulent disease of dogs only, but transmissible via clothing and footwear. The virus is resistant to most disinfectants and can remain alive up to a year in a house or kennel.

The disease causes depression, severe and prolonged vomiting, abdominal pain, and profuse diarrhoea with blood. Urgent vigorous, intensive treatment is necessary for several days, and the

71

illness is often fatal.

Vaccination with live attenuated CPV is effective, and a yearly booster recommended.

Distemper

This is a virus disease transmitted from dog to dog, still common in dog pounds. Initially it presents like a cold — runny eyes, a cough, poor appetite and diarrhoea, followed some weeks later by nervous signs, muscle twitching, fits and paralysis. It may be accompanied by hyperkeratosis of the pads (hard pad).

This disease is often fatal but dedicated nursing can bring success. Your puppy should be vaccinated at 10 and 12 weeks and receive an annual booster.

Canine adenovirus infections

(a) Infectious hepatitis (canine adenovirus type, 1 CAV-1) This is another highly infectious viral disease, associated with nephritis (inflammation of the kidneys), eye disease, and liver damage. Infection is contracted from faeces and urine (recovered dogs may excrete the virus for six months). Puppies in their first year of life are most commonly affected, but dogs of any age are susceptible. Severely affected dogs die in as little as six to eight days. Blue eyes may be seen in the recovery stage.

There is also a respiratory form of this disease which is not so serious.
(b) Canine adenovirus type 2 (CAV-2) This virus is implicated in some cases of contagious respiratory disease.

Vaccination against both illnesses is achieved by giving modified CAV 2 virus, and is boosted yearly.

Leptospirosis

(a) The liver form (Leptospirosis icterohaemorrhagiae)
A bacterial disease of dogs that can be passed to people, transmitted by rats and rat urine. The disease is characterised by sudden onset of fever, jaundice and severe depression. There may also be thirst, vomiting and bloody diarrhoea. Death may occur in two to three hours, but antibiotics give

early and supportive treatment can be successful. Vaccination is effective and a yearly booster should be given.
(b) The kidney form. (Leptospirosis canicola)
A similar bacterial disease, again infectious to man. This illness is transmitted via urine, and hence its name 'lamp-post disease'. Vomiting, depression and inflammation of the mouth with abdominal pain are the main symptoms. Antibiotics and supportive treatment are effective and vaccination with yearly boosters protective.

Kennel cough (infectious rhinotracheitis)

This is a condition caused by a cocktail of viruses and bacteria. Total protection against the disease may not yet be possible, but vaccines are available which give some protection. These are advisable before showing or kennelling. Their effectiveness may only last for six months.

COMMON AILMENTS AND DISEASES

Bowel conditions

The most common illness of your pet will be vomiting or diarrhoea, caused by infections, poisons, parasites, allergies and foreign bodies.

Initial starvation for 24 hours, with limited fluid intake, will control most cases, followed by small meals of boiled white meat. If vomiting is severe or the condition persists or blood is present, consult your veterinarian and aid him or her with a faecal sample. You may have caused the illness yourself by changing the diet or over indulging your pet.

Fits

Fits occur for many reasons and are very frightening to the owner. If they occur, put the dog in a quiet, darkened room. They usually last a short time, and urination and defaecation may occur. Take care not to be bitten.

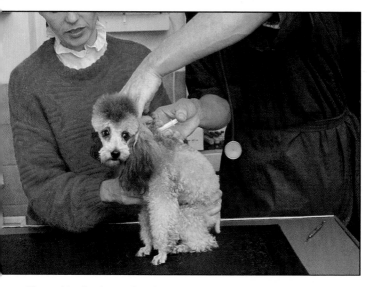

Above: *Vaccination against the common diseases can be combined in two injections at 10 and 12 weeks, with yearly boosters.*

Below: *The veterinarian will, as a matter of course, check the Poodle's heart and lungs for signs of respiratory or heart disease.*

Epileptic dogs become rigid then start paddling their legs. If prolonged fits occur or the dog goes from one fit into another, urgent veterinary help will be needed.

Violent twitching episodes in puppies can be normal. Causes other than epilepsy can be brain tumours, poisons, distemper, liver disease, hydrocephalus and rabies.

Heart disease
Defects of the heart muscle or valves will lead to problems. Symptoms may be coughing, difficulty in breathing, especially during exercise, loss of weight, abdominal distension or weakness.

Management, diet and drugs can prolong life in what are progressive diseases.

The most common heart disease in the Toy and Miniature Poodle is valvular disease. Such dogs can live a number of years if well treated.

Heatstroke
Collapse or coma can be caused by excess heat, usually from leaving dogs in a car in direct sunlight. Cold water and ice cubes are essential, quickly.

Kidney disease
Kidney disease is any impairment of normal kidney function and is one of the most common medical problems of dogs, particularly older ones. There are many causes, and your veterinarian will need to test urine and blood before advising the best treatment and management. With proper management, most pets can live a relatively normal life. Water should always be available but it may be necessary to ration the supply to small amounts given frequently.

Obesity
Obesity is the most common nutritional disease of pets caused by excess fatty tissue. It is more common in advancing age and in females.

Obesity will reduce an animal's enjoyment of life and its owners appreciation of it. More specifically:
1 It predisposes the animal to heart and liver disease
2 Increases the incidence of diabetes
3 Exacerbates arthritis and skin disease
4 Increases surgical risk

Overfeeding of puppies predisposes them to obesity for life, because fat cells grow larger. A strict feeding regime is essential. Keep a regular check.

If your pet has an obesity problem, do not feed anything more than the amount of food prescribed by your veterinarian. Engage the support of the whole

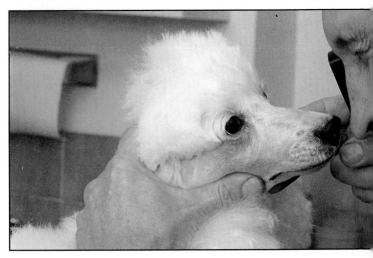

family — no-one must give it extra tit-bits. Specific prescription diets are now available to save preparing complicated meals.

SPECIFIC BREED PROBLEMS

It is advisable to be aware of the common congenital and hereditary defects seen in various breeds of dogs before you buy one, and discuss them with the breeder. Fortunately, breeders are becoming more aware of these conditions, and schemes are being introduced to eradicate them, especially PRA (see below).

I will list the conditions recognised in Poodles in order of frequency.

PRA

This is generalised Progressive Retinal Atrophy, causing a degeneration of the retina and leading to total, incurable blindness. Cataracts may occur when this disease is well advanced, and in such cases cataract surgery will not restore vision. Specialists can spot this condition early with an electro retinogram. Any dogs

---

Below: *A veterinarian is checking the internal structure of the eye for any problems with the aid of an opthalmoscope.*

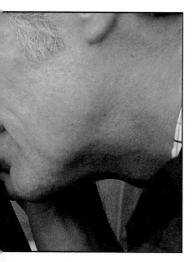

failing this eye test should not be bred from at any time.

Patella luxation (slipping stifle)

This deformity is seen in the Miniature and Toy Poodle, and often needs surgical correction. It has a polygenic pattern of inheritance, but one would counsel against breeding from afflicted animals.

Cryptorchidism

This is the absence of one or both testicles in the scrotum. There is some doubt as to whether one or more genes are involved, but in any event it is sensible not to breed from any dog that has only one testicle.

Entropion

This is the turning in of an eyelid. The condition will cause the Poodle some pain and requires surgical correction.

Von Perthes disease

This is due to a failure of the blood supply to the hip during growth, and leads to a painful lameness. It is seen in Miniature and Toy Poodles. There is evidence of familial predisposition, and surgical treatment is often necessary.

Distichiasis

The dog has extra hairs on lid margin. These hairs cause discomfort and excess tear fluid production, and sometimes need surgical removal.

Other inherited conditions less often seen are congenitally dislocating shoulders, partial alopechia (lack of hair on two-thirds of the body), patent ductus arteriosus (an abnormality of the circulatory system), epilepsy, tracheal collapse (a defective windpipe) and glaucoma (a swollen eye causing much pain).

Such a list is presented not to put you off Poodles — a similar list can be presented for most breeds — but to make you aware of the potential problems, and to guard against breeding from afflicted animals.

Chapter Six

BREEDING

Basic principles
Mating
Whelping
After-care of puppies
The nursing bitch
Puppy progression
Weaning
Neutering

BASIC PRINCIPLES

The pedigree

A pedigree is of value only if knowledge of the qualities of the dogs named therein is available, especially over the last three or four generations. This knowledge can be difficult for the novice breeder to acquire. If the pedigree contains one or more champions, most established breeders will remember them, thereby enabling the novice breeder to gain at least a little knowledge about which breeding lines would suit his or her bitch for the reproduction of a desirable litter.

In-breeding

In-breeding is limited to son to mother, father to daughter, half-brother to half-sister and, closest of all, brother to sister.

In-breeding concentrates good features and bad faults. It can strengthen dominant characteristics and reveal recessive characteristics giving the breeder control in combining and balancing similar genetic factors. In-breeding is not considered to produce any degeneration; it simply concentrates faults and weaknesses already present, thus enabling the breeder to recognise and eradicate them. It is vitally important when in-breeding to choose animals which are as near perfect as possible. In-breeding creates neither faults nor perfections; it simply fixes them in the progeny.

Line-breeding

This entails the selection of breeding stock which has one or more common ancestors of outstanding worth. This method of breeding has brought the most success in breeding programmes; it is relatively safe. Line-breeding to the best individual animals will help to improve the strain.

Outcross breeding

This practice involves the mating of dogs who, in the last five or six generations, are without any common ancestor in their pedigrees.

A dog's genetic worth

All puppies receive 50 per cent of germ plasm from each parent. Without understanding something of the genetic picture of any chosen dog, it is difficult to obtain any specific results. But by delving into the genetic ancestry of the dog, we are able to evaluate the dog's genetic worth as a whole. Unseen genotype, consisting of pairs of genes for each characteristic — which can be dominant or recessive or one of each (in which case the dominant gene is expressed) - add up to a pattern of heredity. We can see the dog's dominant traits as it matures. Good or bad, they are visible. Recessive traits are not always visible. A dominant trait when bred to a dog depicting the same trait will usually breed true and most of the progeny will show this dominant trait. A recessive trait bred to a dog depicting the same trait will result in all offspring exhibiting the recessive trait. A recessive gene cannot be lost; a dominant gene can.

The table opposite details, in my

——— Dominant traits———	——Recessive traits——
Affect a large number of the progeny	Can skip a generation
Are carried only by the affected animals	The recessive gene must be produced by both sire and dam
Will reduce any danger of continuing any unwanted traits	A dog carrying a pair of recessive genes will exhibit the trait
Never skip a generation	A dog carrying only one gene will not
Will guarantee the breeding pattern	

─── Desirable traits ───	─── Undesirable traits ───
Long muzzle (R)	Short muzzle (D)
Lean cheeks (R)	Heavy cheeks (D)
Chiselling (D)	Lack of chiselling (R)
Lean skull (R)	Apple headed (D)
Low ear set (R)	High ear set (D)
Long ears (R)	Small ears (D)
Oval eyes (R)	Large round eye (D)
Dark eyes (D)	Light eye (R)
Scissor bite (D)	Undershot (R)
Long neck (R)	Overshot (R)
Short back (D)	Lack of neck (D)
Well laid shoulder (R)	Long back (R)
Good patellas (D)	Upright shoulder (D)
Arched feet and Thick pads (D)	Slipping patellas
Dense coat (D)	Thin splayed feet (R)
A Black (D)	Thin silky coat (R)
White coat (R)	
Brown coat (R)	
Apricot and Silver coat (R)	

opinion, desirable and undesirable traits in the Poodle, and whether these are dominant or recessive. Note that the desired points can be a combination of dominants and recessives.

Below: *A Miniature and Toy Poodle of about the same age with the Silver showing on the faces. Note the well-shaped eyes and good length of foreface. Both dogs show promise for the future.*

The novice breeder

I would like to begin with a warning that breeding dogs is not a matter for the novice or pet owner. When you buy a bitch as a pet that is what she should remain, not to become a brood bitch. The responsibility for the welfare and quality of pedigree dogs should remain in the hands of dedicated and knowledgeable breeders. No novice can assess the genetic background of dogs or bitches sold as pets. Therefore it is quite impossible for pet owners to know when they mate their bitch to a friend or neighbour's dog, whether such a mating will produce sound and healthy puppies.

Another important point to bear in mind is that puppies from three weeks old, until they go to their new owners when they are eight weeks of age, will require much time and attention. They need to be fed at least four times a day. You can be sure that once weaning has commenced the bitch will stop keeping her puppies clean - another chore which you will have to undertake.

However if, after these warnings, you particularly wish your bitch to have a litter you would be wise to consult her breeder who will be able to advise you on a suitable stud dog, and will usually be able to assist with the sale of the puppies.

A Standard Poodle bitch will, on average, produce eight puppies in a litter; the Miniature bitch produces an average of four to five puppies per litter and the Toy bitch on average three puppies per litter.

MATING

Miniature and Toy Poodles come into season when quite young, usually at the age of six months. Standards, who take longer to mature, have their first season

Gestation table

Jan	Mar	Feb	Apr	Mar	May	Apr	June	May	Jul	Jun	Aug
1 due 4		1 due 4		1 due 2		1 due 2		1 due 2		1 due 2	
2 due 5		2 due 5		2 due 3		2 due 3		2 due 3		2 due 3	
3 due 6		3 due 6		3 due 4		3 due 4		3 due 4		3 due 4	
4 due 7		4 due 7		4 due 5		4 due 5		4 due 5		4 due 5	
5 due 8		5 due 8		5 due 6		5 due 6		5 due 6		5 due 6	
6 due 9		6 due 9		6 due 7		6 due 7		6 due 7		6 due 7	
7 due 10		7 due 10		7 due 8		7 due 8		7 due 8		7 due 8	
8 due 11		8 due 11		8 due 9		8 due 9		8 due 9		8 due 9	
9 due 12		9 due 12		9 due 10		9 due 10		9 due 10		9 due 10	
10 due 13		10 due 13		10 due 11		10 due 11		10 due 11		10 due 11	
11 due 14		11 due 14		11 due 12		11 due 12		11 due 12		11 due 12	
12 due 15		12 due 15		12 due 13		12 due 13		12 due 13		12 due 13	
13 due 16		13 due 16		13 due 14		13 due 14		13 due 14		13 due 14	
14 due 17		14 due 17		14 due 15		14 due 15		14 due 15		14 due 15	
15 due 18		15 due 18		15 due 16		15 due 16		15 due 16		15 due 16	
16 due 19		16 due 19		16 due 17		16 due 17		16 due 17		16 due 17	
17 due 20		17 due 20		17 due 18		17 due 18		17 due 18		17 due 18	
18 due 21		18 due 21		18 due 19		18 due 19		18 due 19		18 due 19	
19 due 22		19 due 22		19 due 20		19 due 20		19 due 20		19 due 20	
20 due 23		20 due 23		20 due 21		20 due 21		20 due 21		20 due 21	
21 due 24		21 due 24		21 due 22		21 due 22		21 due 22		21 due 22	
22 due 25		22 due 25		22 due 23		22 due 23		22 due 23		22 due 23	
23 due 26		23 due 26		23 due 24		23 due 24		23 due 24		23 due 24	
24 due 27		24 due 27		24 due 25		24 due 25		24 due 25		24 due 25	
25 due 28		25 due 28		25 due 26		25 due 26		25 due 26		25 due 26	
26 due 29		26 due 29		26 due 27		26 due 27		26 due 27		26 due 27	
27 due 30		27 due 30		27 due 28		27 due 28		27 due 28		27 due 28	
28 due 31		28 due 1 May		28 due 29		28 due 29		28 due 29		28 due 29	
29 due 1 Apr				29 due 30		29 due 30		29 due 30		29 due 30	
30 due 2 Apr				30 due 31		30 due 1 July		30 due 31		30 due 31	
31 due 3 Apr				31 due 1 June				31 due 1 Aug			

somewhat later, at about ten months. Both six months and ten months are considered far too young for mating; bitches should not be allowed to rear a litter before they are fully mature. By the

Above: *White Poodle puppies with the face and feet clipped. White Poodles often have a little pale Apricot on the ears when they are young, but this normally fades as the dog matures.*

Table based on 63 days inclusive of both dates, leap years not allowed for.

Jul	Sept	Aug	Oct	Sept	Nov	Oct	Dec	Nov	Jan	Dec	Feb
1 due 1		1 due 2		1 due 2		1 due 2		1 due 2		1 due 1	
2 due 2		2 due 3		2 due 3		2 due 3		2 due 3		2 due 2	
3 due 3		3 due 4		3 due 4		3 due 4		3 due 4		3 due 3	
4 due 4		4 due 5		4 due 5		4 due 5		4 due 5		4 due 4	
5 due 5		5 due 6		5 due 6		5 due 6		5 due 6		5 due 5	
6 due 6		6 due 7		6 due 7		6 due 7		6 due 7		6 due 6	
7 due 7		7 due 8		7 due 8		7 due 8		7 due 8		7 due 7	
8 due 8		8 due 9		8 due 9		8 due 9		8 due 9		8 due 8	
9 due 9		9 due 10		9 due 10		9 due 10		9 due 10		9 due 9	
10 due 10		10 due 11		10 due 11		10 due 11		10 due 11		10 due 10	
11 due 11		11 due 12		11 due 12		11 due 12		11 due 12		11 due 11	
12 due 12		12 due 13		12 due 13		12 due 13		12 due 13		12 due 12	
13 due 13		13 due 14		13 due 14		13 due 14		13 due 14		13 due 13	
14 due 14		14 due 15		14 due 15		14 due 15		14 due 15		14 due 14	
15 due 15		15 due 16		15 due 16		15 due 16		15 due 16		15 due 15	
16 due 16		16 due 17		16 due 17		16 due 17		16 due 17		16 due 16	
17 due 17		17 due 18		17 due 18		17 due 18		17 due 18		17 due 17	
18 due 18		18 due 19		18 due 19		18 due 19		18 due 19		18 due 18	
19 due 19		19 due 20		19 due 20		19 due 20		19 due 20		19 due 19	
20 due 20		20 due 21		20 due 21		20 due 21		20 due 21		20 due 20	
21 due 21		21 due 22		21 due 22		21 due 22		21 due 22		21 due 21	
22 due 22		22 due 23		22 due 23		22 due 23		22 due 23		22 due 22	
23 due 23		23 due 24		23 due 24		23 due 24		23 due 24		23 due 23	
24 due 24		24 due 25		24 due 25		24 due 25		24 due 25		24 due 24	
25 due 25		25 due 26		25 due 26		25 due 26		25 due 26		25 due 25	
26 due 26		26 due 27		26 due 27		26 due 27		26 due 27		26 due 26	
27 due 27		27 due 28		27 due 28		27 due 28		27 due 28		27 due 27	
28 due 28		28 due 29		28 due 29		28 due 29		28 due 29		28 due 28	
29 due 29		29 due 30		29 due 30		29 due 30		29 due 30		29 due 1 Mar	
30 due 30		30 due 31		30 due 1 Dec		30 due 31		30 due 31		30 due 2 Mar	
31 due 1 Oct		31 due 1 Nov				31 due 1 Jan				31 due 3 Mar	

When mating your bitch, do allow time for her to make friends with the dog. A good stud will know how to flirt and coerce the bitch to accept such a charming and attractive dog.

When the bitch is ready, she will stand motionless, tail askew. The dog will mount and insert his penis into the bitch's vulva.

Afer a minute or so, the dog will move, lifting one leg over the bitch's back to form the tie.

second season, both Miniature and Toy bitches are usually mature enough for maternal duties. With the Standard it is wiser to wait at least another six months. Many Standard breeders prefer to wait until their bitches are at least two years of age. The bitch's normal mating cycle lasts approximately 21 days. During the first 10 days there is a bright red discharge from the vulva which will gradually fade to pale pink and then to cream. This discharge will last until the 10th or 11th day. From then until the 18th day the bitch will normally stand and accept the dog.

Times vary with individual bitches; some will even accept a stud as early as the 4th day and as late as the 20th day, but the 11th day is usually considered the best.

As soon as the bitch comes into season you must book an appointment with the owner of the stud dog. A maiden bitch should

The bulbous gland at the base of the dog's penis swells during mating preventing withdrawal, hence what is known as the tie.

always be mated to an experienced stud. Two novices can make the mating difficult, prolonging the act to such an extent that both dog and bitch become quite exhausted.

The 'tie'

Once the dog has mounted the bitch and ejaculation occurs, the dog and the bitch are 'tied'. This occurs when the bitch's vulva constricts the male's engorged penis. The 'tie' can last up to 30 minutes — the reason for this is quite unknown, as it is possible for a bitch to conceive without any 'tie' at all. During the 'tie' both dog and bitch should be carefully controlled. A bitch attacking the dog at this time could cause much damage.

When the mating is completed, the dog and bitch should be separated. Both can then be given a drink, allowed to relieve themselves and then to rest.

Care of the pregnant bitch

Directly after mating, the bitch should be wormed. This can reduce the risk of high infestation of the puppies. Extra food is not essential until the 5th week, when a daily dietary supplement is required for the foetal development of the puppies. Small quantities of calcium, iron, phosphorus and vitamins should be added to the bitch's food. At this time she should be fed on her own, taking care to keep to the same feeding times each day. Two smaller meals instead of one large helping are more acceptable when she is heavily in whelp.

Gentle exercise is necessary, especially during the early weeks of her pregnancy. With a normal size litter it should be possible to tell by the 30th day, with the swelling of the abdomen, that she is in whelp. With a small litter there will be little

sign until she is nearer to the time of whelping.

WHELPING

By using the gestation table on pages 80-81, it is possible to prepare for your bitch's whelping well in advance. Poodles are on the whole very easy whelpers, but the bitch should be provided with a whelping box (see below) which she can become accustomed to well before her time. The whelping box should preferably be somewhere where the bitch's

Below: *This is a good, ready-made whelping kennel. The roof of the kennel is made to slide, and the floor can be taken out for cleaning. A loose front is made to fit on top of a hinged flap which can be dropped down.*

movements can be watched, and also where she can be confined in an enclosure. Otherwise you may find that she will want to carry the puppies all over the house. We find that bitches at this time usually require and prefer a fairly dark bed, which affords her protection from other dogs and disturbances. Towards the end of her time, when she is heavy in whelp, she will appreciate a soft bed to lie on. But as soon as labour commences, all bedding must be removed and the whelping box lined with plenty of newspaper which, as labour commences, she will tear and scratch until it is in shreds. This will help the bitch in labour, and is both hygienic and absorbent.

Equipment
The following is a list of equipment required at a whelping and its uses.

A whelping box This should be prepared in advance. For a Standard Poodle the box should be about 4ft 6in (1.4m) square with high sides and back. It should have a front opening and preferably a hinged lid. A guard rail placed inside the box around the three sides will prevent the bitch from accidentally squashing a puppy if it crawls behind her. This rail consists of 1in x 3in (2.5 x 7.5cm) wooden slats fastened approximately 4in (10cm) above the floor level. For Miniature and Toys, a box measuring 2ft x 2ft x 18in (61 x 61 x 46cm) should be used with slats 2in (5cm) above floor level.

Several layers of newspaper
These can be constantly changed during whelping.

Rough towelling If the bitch appears to be tiring, once the puppy is protruding it can be gripped by a piece of towelling and gently drawn out and down, but only when the bitch strains.

Box A box with a covered hot water bottle is necessary to put the first puppies in whilst the bitch is dealing with the newest arrival.

An emergency feeder Very occasionally, for various reasons, the bitch will be unable to feed her puppies. To survive, they will need to be hand reared. It is essential that puppies are fed every two hours day and night for the first week at least using a mother's milk replacer (eg *Lactol* or *Whelpi*) freshly mixed and fed according to the manufacturer's instructions. I prefer to use a premature infant tube feeder. These feeders are about 4½ in (11.5cm) long and marked in teaspoon measures with a rubber teat at each end. The small teat is for the puppy to suck; the teat at the other end allows you to control the flow and feed the correct amount, which is most important.

Glucose This should be given to the bitch in milk or milk replacer during whelping and afterwards.

Disinfectant Use to wash your hands before touching puppies.

Sharp clean scissors and strong cotton Bitches usually sever the umbilical cord and clean up, but if she is reluctant to do so, this can be done with scissors, making sure that the flow of blood from the placenta (afterbirth) to the puppy has ceased. Snip the cord ¾ - ½ in (2-4cm) from the puppy and tie tightly with cotton. Do not pull the cord away; you could cause an umbilical hernia.

Cotton lint If the bitch does not release the puppy from its own membraneous sac in which it is born, you must open the sac with your fingers and clean the puppy with the lint or towelling, thereby stimulating it into crying.

Infra-red lamp Suspend the lamp over the whelping box. Puppies must have a high temperature at birth, at least 75-80°F (23.8-26.6°C).
Or

A heating pad This is usually preferred as it gives out heat for the puppies without making the bitch uncomfortable. Care must be taken that the flex is well protected and in a position well out of reach of the bitch and puppies.

Labour
The commencement of labour in the Poodle bitch is usually preceded by roughly 24 hours of restlessness and panting accompanied by

Below: *A week old puppy happily feeding, its paws kneading for milk. Note the flat ears, unopened eye and thick, curly coat.*

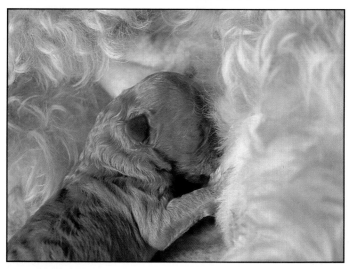

scratching and tearing up the paper in her box. This is normally followed by a rather quiet period. Also at this time, the normal body temperature of 101.5°F (38.6°C) will drop below 99°F (37.2°C). The labour pains will soon occur, rather far apart at first but gradually getting closer together in time, continuing until the water bag, looking rather like a small dark brown balloon, appears. Within an hour at the outside the bag will burst, and shortly after this a puppy should appear. Once the bag has burst, if a puppy has not appeared within an hour it is wise to send for your veterinarian. In the event of labour pains continuing for longer than two hours, or if they appear to be getting weaker, the veterinarian should also be summoned.

Birth
Once the puppy appears, the bitch will turn round breaking the sac and biting the naval cord. She will then eat the sac, the cord and the afterbirth. Sometimes when the cord breaks the afterbirth is left inside the bitch. This will usually be

expelled by the birth of the next puppy. The bitch will continue to clean the puppy until the next puppy is ready to emerge, when the whole process starts again.

Usually bitches are perfectly capable of whelping the litter without any help from you but it is better, especially with a maiden bitch, (ie having her first litter), for you to be present in case of an emergency. Often with the birth of the first puppy the bitch looks quite bemused and it may become necessary for you to remove the sac. The cord joining the puppy to the afterbirth should be tied tightly with cotton, once the blood flow has ceased, and snipped off between the cotton and the afterbirth. The latter, if not already expelled from the bitch, can then be gently pulled out, as the bitch strains, until removed.

Remember that you must never pull the cord away from the puppy as this action can cause an umbilical hernia. Always count the number of afterbirths, checking against the number of puppies, to make sure they have all been expelled.

A bitch will often have several puppies in quick succession, then she will rest before the arrival of the last of the litter. During this time a drink of milk with glucose and

Below: *As puppies fight for the teats, scrambling over one another, it is necessary to ensure that a weaker puppy gets its share.*

honey is usually acceptable.

Once the whelping is over, the bitch should be allowed to rest quietly without disturbance for several hours. Then she must be allowed out to relieve herself and quickly returned to her litter. For the first 24 hours, give mainly liquid feeds: milk with glucose and honey or lightly scrambled egg. Water is essential for the milk supply of the bitch.

On the first day after the whelping, I strongly advise a visit from your veterinarian when the bitch and the puppies can be examined thoroughly and any abnormalities of the whelps can be diagnosed at once.

AFTER-CARE OF PUPPIES

Docking and dew claws

When the puppies are between 4-6 days of age, providing they are strong and healthy the dew claws must be removed and, if desired, the tail docked.

Signs of ill-health

Happy and healthy puppies are always quiet and contented. Puppies that cry a lot are either hungry or cold, but constant crying could be a sign of serious trouble and you should call your veterinarian.

THE NURSING BITCH

While the bitch is feeding her litter it is important to give her plenty of nutritious food, at least three meals of substance a day. Plenty of water is essential.

Below: *Newly-born puppies can crawl on all four legs to their mother although they cannot stand or walk. This is a reflex action.*

Bottom: *Healthy puppies have a strong sucking reflex at birth accompanied by a reflex kneading action in the front legs used to stimulate the bitch's milk.*

Eclampsia

Because of the quick and fatal nature of eclampsia, which can occur at any time but usually between 2-4 weeks regardless of the number of puppies, it is necessary here to state its cause and symptoms. Eclampsia is caused by a lack of calcium in the blood of the nursing bitch. The symptoms are panting, shaking, a somewhat wild expression, a staggering gait, muscular rigidity and restlessness. To save the bitch, it is vital that veterinary assistance is sought immediately as an intravenous injection of calcium is required.

PUPPY PROGRESSION

Weight A puppy should double its birth weight between 8-10 days. It should be weighed daily, and if there is a loss of weight, or no gain for two days, supplementary feeding is a necessity.

Sucking reflex In healthy puppies this is strong at birth. It is weak if

The puppy is abnormal, cold or premature — it is vital to keep the puppies warm (see below).

Body Temperature This should be approximately 94-99°F (34.4-37.2°C) in first two weeks, and 97-100°F (36.1-37.7°C) from two to four weeks. The normal temperature of an adult dog is 101.2°F. This is why it is essential to keep the puppies very warm. The shivering reflex doesn't develop until approximately eight days after birth. Therefore, during the first two weeks of life the temperature in the whelping box should be high, at least 75-80°F (23.8-26-6°C). Normal puppies have a twitching action between one to three weeks. This disappears after they are a month old.

Locomotion Puppies can stand at three weeks, and walk and run at four weeks.

Eyes Their eyes open between 10-16 days; at this time it is essential to protect them against strong light.

Ears Ears open at approximately 13 days. At four weeks, but rarely before, the puppies will recognise their owner.

WEANING

Once the puppies' eyes are open between 10-16 days, they will soon be moving around learning to walk. From this time, get them accustomed to the sound of your voice and being handled.

At approximately 4 weeks of age their milk teeth, 28 in all, begin to erupt and, although they will be

Above left: *A close-up of a four-day old Poodle puppy showing the eyes and ears still tightly closed. The eyes will open between 10 and 16 days old, while the ears will open at approximately 13 days.*

Bottom left: *A four-day old puppy with a well-shaped skull. The tail is still undocked at this stage, and can remain so if desired. It is most important to keep puppies of this early age very warm.*

getting plenty of milk from the bitch, now is the time to start weaning. A little scraped raw beef, fed to them with your fingers, I have found to be the quickest method. Puppies first suck the meat and, once tasted, attack the remainder with relish. A few days later, they should be eating two meat meals a day. Once the puppies are eating the meat easily, they should be introduced to a warm milk meal. This may be cow's milk, goat's milk, which is excellent, or one of the commercial brands especially prepared for dogs. These may all be mixed with a cereal such as corn flakes or oats made into porridge. Once or twice a week, vary the diet with a little scrambled egg. As the puppies mature, well toasted wholemeal bread can be added to both meat and milk meals.

During this weaning period, the mother should be separated from her puppies for longer and longer periods. There is a natural instinct, which can cause distress to the owner: the bitch, as her milk recedes, will quite often, regurgitate her food after she has eaten if allowed near the puppies. Providing she has not eaten any large lumps of meat or biscuit, this will do no harm to the puppies but will necessitate feeding the bitch again. It is wiser to keep the bitch from her puppies for at least an hour after she has eaten.

Once the puppies are completely weaned, they should be fed from

Veterinary advice on neutering

As we already know, bitches have periodic seasons (heat or oestrus) when they are able to receive the male. During this time they loose blood-stained fluid and this can be messy in the house. It usually lasts for three weeks and occurs twice a year. False pregnancy may follow two months after a heat, with a change in the bitch's temperature, signs of nest-making, lack of appetite, and possibly ill-temper if disturbed. During the height of her season, the bitch may make every attempt to escape from her home to find a mate of any size or breed.

Oral suppression of heat can be achieved with contraceptive pills or injections. Discuss their relative uses and merits with your veterinarian. They may be useful for limited periods, but complications include diabetes, weight gain, shorter gaps between heat and possibly the increased incidence of milk gland tumours.

Heat and false pregnancy problems can best be prevented by surgical removal of the uterus and ovaries. It is a major operation but one that is routinely done. Recovery is within a week, and the operation is usually carried out midway between seasons.

Benefits
The neutering of bitches should be strongly considered if you do not wish to breed. If not neutered, your pet will be more or less out of action for six weeks of the year because of season, and will often display the symptoms associated with false pregnancy. There will be less chance of breast tumours (some of which are malignant) later in life, and emergency hysterectomy, due to an infected womb, will never be required if your bitch is neutered.

After-effects
Character change should not occur. Most changes are related to weight gain following surgery, which you must not allow to occur. Bitches do tend to take less exercise after neutering, so **less** food should be given than prior to surgery.

Neutering of males
Male dogs do not have seasonal sexual activity, but are active throughout the year. Oversexed or aggressive males may need to be castrated or given drugs to suppress masculine activity. Again, injudicious feeding can cause weight gain following neutering.

separate dishes enabling you to know how much each puppy consumes and check that all are eating well. Quantities will vary with the size and appetite of each puppy. Feed about every four hours, three meals of meat or puppy meal and two of puppy biscuit, wholemeal bread, or cereal moistened with milk or broth.

Above: *When weaning puppies, it is far easier to start with a little scraped raw beef fed with your fingers. The puppies will first suck the meat and once tasted will eat with relish. This older puppy still enjoys this method.*

Worming
Puppies should be treated for roundworms at two and a half to three weeks of age and subsequently at two-week intervals up to the age of three months using medication advised by your veterinarian. See pages 37 and 44 for advice on worming and the treatment of other parasites in the older dog.

Chapter Seven

SHOWING YOUR POODLE

The Breed Standards
Choosing a show puppy
Training for the show ring
The show systems
Crufts Dog Show

THE BREED STANDARDS

A Standard endeavours to describe in words an ideal specimen of the breed, to provide a basis for assessment in the show ring. As a word 'picture' however, it is subject to many interpretations by judges and exhibitors.

The Poodle Standard is identical for all three sizes. The Miniature and Toy should be in every respect a replica, in Miniature and Toy, of the Standard Poodle, except on the required size — see UK and US official standards that follow, which differ slightly on size.

The UK Standard

This is reproduced by the kind permission of the Kennel Club.

General appearance Well balanced, elegant looking with very proud carriage.

Characteristics Distinguished by a special type of clip for show activity and by a type of coat which does not moult.

Temperament Gay spirited and good tempered.

Head and skull Long and fine with slight peak. Skull not broad, moderate stop. Foreface strong, well chiselled, not falling away under eyes; cheek bones and muscles flat. Lips tight fitting. Chin well defined but not protruding. Head in proportion to size of dog.

Eyes Almond shaped, dark, not set too close together, full of fire and intelligence.

Ears Leather long and wide, set low, hanging close to face.

Mouth Jaws strong with perfect, regular, complete scissor bite, ie the upper teeth closely overlapping the lower teeth and set square to

Below: *Ch Montravia Tommy Gun, Best in Show at Crufts 1985, UK Dog Of The Year 1984. Compare him with the skeleton — perfection!*

Skeleton

1 Nasal bones 2 Orbit 3 Zygomatic arch 4 Sagittal crest 5 Occiput 6 Upper jaw or maxilla 7 Atlas 8 Axis 9 Cervical or Neck bones 10 Scapula 11 Point of shoulder 12 Humerus or Upperarm 13 Radius and Ulna or Forearm 14 Carpel 15 Sternum 16 Metacarpus 17 Ribs 18 Vertebrae 19 Pelvis 20 Sacrum 21 Coccygeal or Tail bone 22 Ischium or Hip bone 23 Femur 24 Tibia 25 Tarsal or Hock bone 26 Metatasus 27 Patella 28 Phalanges

Conformation points

A Muzzle B Stop C Skull D Lips E Flews F Withers G Shoulder H Loin I Rump J Stifle or Knee K Hock L Brisket M Elbow N Wrist O Pastern P Cheeks.

The blue rules illustrate the desired Poodle conformation — a squarely built body and the correct angulation of the fore and hindquarters, with the correct outline of the English Saddle Clip.

Below: *View of the Poodle's head as seen from above showing the desired proportions of muzzle to skull — the length from the occiput to the stop is about the same as the length of the muzzle.*

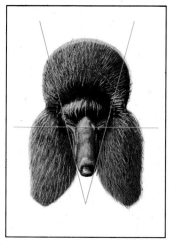

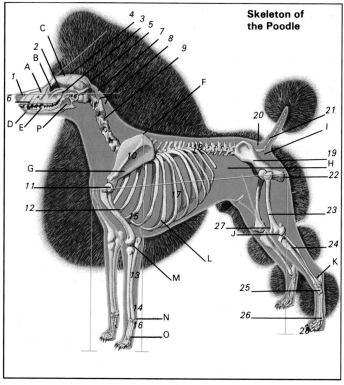

Skeleton of the Poodle

the jaws. A full set of 42 teeth is desirable.

Neck Well proportioned, of good length and strong to admit of the head being carried high and with dignity. Skin fitting tightly at the throat.

Forequarters Well laid back shoulders, strong and muscular. Legs set straight from shoulders, well muscled.

Body Chest deep and moderately wide. Ribs well sprung and rounded. Back short and strong, slightly hollowed; loins broad and muscular.

Hindquarters Thighs well developed and muscular; well bent stifles, hocks well let down; hind legs turning neither in nor out.

Feet Tight, proportionately small, oval in shape, turning neither in nor out, toes arched, pads thick and hard, well cushioned. Pasterns strong.

Tail Set on rather high, carried at slight angle away from body, never curled or carried over back, thick at root. Customarily docked.

Gait/movement Sound, free and light movement essential with plenty of drive.

Coat Very profuse and dense; of good harsh texture. All short hair close, thick and curly. It is strongly recommended that the traditional Lion Clip be adhered to.

Colour All solid colours. White and creams to have black nose, lips and eyerims, black toenails desirable; browns to have dark amber eyes, dark liver nose, lips, eyerims and toenails. Apricots to have dark eyes with black points or deep amber eyes with liver points. Blacks, silvers and blues to have black nose, lips, eyerims and toenails. Creams, apricots, browns, silvers and blues may show varying shades of the same colour up to 18 months. Clear colours preferred.

Size Standard — over 38cm (15ins). Miniature — height at shoulder should be under 38cm (15ins) but not under 28cm (11ins). Toy — height at shoulder should be under 28cm (11ins).

Faults Any departure from the foregoing points should be considered a fault and the seriousness with which the fault should be regarded should be in exact proportion to its degree. Note: Male animals should have two apparently normal testicles fully descended into the scrotum.

Notes on the Standard Characteristics The special types of clips are the English Saddle Lion Clip, the Continental Lion Clip or, for Poodles under one year, the Puppy Clip.

Tail A tail carried over the back completely spoils the overall balance and topline of the Poodle.

Forequarters Without a well-laid sloping shoulder, a sound and free movement is impossible.

Hindquarters With the propelling force of the dog coming largely from the rear quarters, well muscled thighs and good angulation are important.

The US Standard
This is reproduced by kind permission of the American Kennel Club.

General Appearance, carriage and condition That of a very active, intelligent and elegant-appearing dog, squarely built, well proportioned, moving soundly and carrying himself proudly. Properly clipped in the traditional fashion and carefully groomed, the Poodle has about him an air of distinction and dignity peculiar to himself.

Head and expression (a) Skull Moderately rounded, with a slight but definite stop. Cheekbones and muscles flat. Length from occiput to stop about the same as length of muzzle. **(b) Muzzle** Long, straight and fine, with slight chiselling under the eyes. Strong without lippiness.

Right: The beautiful character of the Poodle's head, eye and typical expression is completely lost when the head is too coarse, the eyes round and staring and the muzzle too broad as in the top picture. Below, this closely clipped Poodle's ears are too high set; the base should be level with corner of eye.

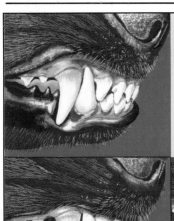

Bites

On the left is the correct 'scissor' bite; the top teeth fit over the bottom teeth. Below left shows the incorrect 'level' bite where the front teeth meet top to top. Below shows the 'undershot' mouth. This is also an incorrect bite. In this case the lower teeth go in front of the top teeth.

The chin definite enough to preclude snipiness. Teeth white, strong and with a scissor bite.
(c) Eyes Very dark, oval in shape and set far enough and positioned to create an alert intelligent expression **(d) Ears** Hanging close to head, set at or slightly below eye level. The ear leather is long, wide, and thickly feathered; ear fringe should be of excessive length.
Neck and shoulders Neck well

proportioned, strong and long enough to permit the head to be carried high and with dignity. Skin snug at throat. The neck rises from strong, smoothly muscled shoulders. The shoulder blade is

Below: *On the far left, well-angulated rear legs; middle and right legs are incorrect being too straight in stifle and hocks.*

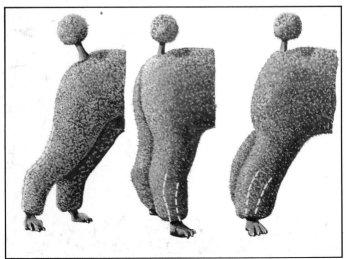

well laid back and approximately the same length as the upper foreleg.

Body To insure the desirable squarely-built appearance, the length of body measured from the breastbone to the point of the rump approximates the height from the highest point of the shoulders to the ground. **(a) Chest** Deep and moderately wide with well sprung ribs. **(b) Back** The topline is level, neither sloping nor roached, from the highest point of the shoulder blade to the base of the tail, with the exception of a slight hollow just behind the shoulder. The loin is short, broad, and muscular.

Tail Straight, set on high and carried up, docked of sufficient

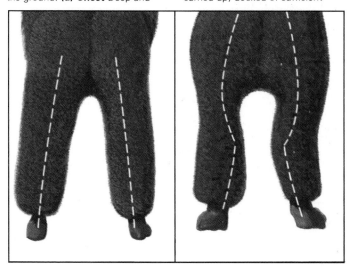

Above: *Left shows correct rear legs parallel from hips to feet. Right shows cow-hocks; when moving the legs will nearly touch at hocks.*

Below: *This Poodle is incorrect in the following ways — lack of neck, bad, rising top-line and a too-high set of the tail.*

length to insure a balanced outline.
Legs (a) Forelegs Straight and
parallel when viewed from the
front. When viewed from the side
the elbow is directly below the
highest point of the shoulder. The
pasterns are strong. Bone and
muscle of both forelegs and
hindlegs are in proportion to size of
dog. **(b) Hindlegs** Straight and
parallel when viewed from the rear.
Muscular with width in the region
of the stifles which are well bent;
femur and tibia are about equal in
length; hock to heel short and
perpendicular to the ground. When
standing, the rear toes are only
slightly behind the point of rump.
The angulation of the hindquarters
balances that of the forequarters.
Feet The feet are rather small, oval
in shape with toes well arched and
cushioned on thick firm pads. Nails
short but not excessively
shortened. The feet turn neither in
nor out. Dew claws may be
removed.
Coat
(a) Quality (1) curly: of naturally
harsh texture, dense throughout
(2) corded: hanging in tight even
cords of varying length; longer on
mane or body coat, head and ears;
shorter on puffs, bracelets, and

pompoms. **(b) clip** A Poodle under
12 months may be shown in the
'puppy' clip. In all regular classes,
Poodles 12 months or over must be
shown in the 'English Saddle' or
'Continental' clip. In the Stud Dog
and Brood Bitch classes and in a
non-competitive Parade of
Champions, Poodles may be shown
in the 'Sporting' clip. A Poodle
shown in any other type of clip
shall be disqualified.
Colour The coat is an even and
solid colour at the skin. In blues,
greys, silvers, browns, cafe-au-laits,
apricots, and creams the coat may
show varying shades of the same
colour. This is frequently present in
the somewhat darker feathering of
the ears and in the tipping of the
ruff. While clear colours are
definitely preferred, such natural
variation in the shading of the coat
is not to be considered a fault.
Brown and cafe-au-lait Poodles
have liver-coloured noses, eyerims
and lips, dark toenails and dark
amber eyes. Black, blue, grey,

Below: *This lovely Apricot Toy
Poodle has a good coat colour.
Some variation in the shade of the
colour over the coat is permitted.*

silver, cream and white Poodles have black noses, eyerims and lips, black or self-coloured toenails and very dark eyes. In the apricots while the foregoing colouring is preferred, liver-coloured noses, eyerims and lips, and amber eyes are permitted but are not desirable.

Parti-coloured dogs shall be disqualified. The coat of a parti-coloured dog is not an even solid colour at the skin but is of two or more colours.

Gait A straightforward trot with light springy action and strong hindquarters drive. Head and tail carried up. Sound effortless movement is essential.

Size

The Standard Poodle is over 15 inches at the highest point of the shoulders. Any Poodle which is 15 inches or less in height shall be disqualified from competition as a Standard Poodle.

The Miniature Poodle is 15 inches or under at the highest point of the shoulders, with a minimum height in excess of 10 inches. Any Poodle which is over 15 inches or is 10 inches or less at the highest point of the shoulders shall be disqualified from competition as a Miniature Poodle.

The Toy Poodle is 10 inches or under at the highest point of the shoulders. Any Poodle which is more than 10 inches at the highest point of the shoulders shall be disqualified from competition as a Toy Poodle.

As long as the Toy Poodle is definitely a Toy Poodle, and the Miniature Poodle a Miniature, both in balance and proportion for the variety, diminutiveness shall be the deciding factor when all other points are equal.

Value of points
General appearance, temperament, carriage and condition: 30
Head, expression, ears, eyes, and teeth: 20
Body, neck, legs, feet and tail: 20
Gait: 20
Coat, colour and texture: 10

Major Faults Any distinct deviation from the desired characteristics described in the

Below top: This shows incorrect feet, turning out with toes that are unattractively open and spreading.

Below middle: An excellent front with the correct width between straight, parallel forelegs and good, tight, oval-shaped feet.

Below bottom: This Poodle's front is undesirable for showing purposes. The distance between the forelegs is far too wide.

101

Breed Standard with particular attention to the following:

Temperament Shyness or sharpness

Muzzle Undershot, overshot, wry mouth, lack of chin.

Eyes Round, protruding, large or very light.

Pigment Colour of nose, lips and eyerims incomplete, or of wrong colour for colour of dog.

Neck and shoulders Ewe neck, steep shoulders.

Tail Set low, curled, or carried over the back.

Hindquarters Cow hocks.

Feet Paper or splayfoot.

Disqualifications

Clip A dog in any type of clip other than those listed under Coat shall be disqualified.

Parti-colours The coat of a parti-coloured dog is not an even solid colour at the skin but of two or more colours. Parti- coloured dogs shall be disqualified.

Size A dog over or under the height limits specified shall be disqualified.

CHOOSING A SHOW PUPPY

It is practically impossible to choose a young puppy of eight to ten weeks with the certainty that it will mature into a top quality show Poodle. The best you can do is to choose a puppy of show potential from a breeder of repute chosen with the help, if possible, of another well-established breeder.

Firstly, do ask to see the dam of the litter from which you are making your selection. Make sure the whole litter is of a friendly nature, looking healthy and happy. It is a good idea to ask the breeder to divide the sexes, and for a short while just study the puppies of the sex you require. Take note of their movement and general behaviour as they are playing. Look for good, overall balance, ie length of the body equal to height at the withers giving a square outline. A good reach of neck and high head carriage are essential in a future show specimen.

Close examination

Stand the puppy on a table for a closer examination. The muzzle at this age should give a slightly curved effect, rather like a 'Roman' nose. The base of the ear should be set level with the eyes, and the leathers of the ear should be thick and long. Eyes in all Poodles should have a bright and intelligent expression. They should be dark brown in Blacks, Whites and Silvers, and dark amber in Browns. Apricots have dark brown or amber eyes. All Poodles should have almond-shaped eyes; a light, round eye is undesirable. A scissor bite is essential, the teeth white and even

Left: *This lovely head study illustrates the desired qualities of the Poodle's eye — almond-shaped, dark, full of fire and intelligence.*

with tight lips. The tail should be set on high, carried at a slight angle away from the body. It must not curl or be carried over the back.

The feet should be tight and oval in shape with well-cushioned pads. The front legs must be straight with no looseness at the elbow. The back legs should have a good bend of stifle with well let down hocks. If purchasing a male, ascertain that the puppy is entire with two testicles descended into the scrotum.

An old standard

The following standard, taken from Dr Gordon Staples' RN book 'Our Friend the Dog', published by Dean & Sons Ltd, London, in 1883, was adopted by the Poodle Club in England soon after its formation in 1876. It makes a fascinating comparision with the present-day standards for the UK and US.

This standard of points has two sections, 'The Perfect Black Poodle' and 'The Perfect Red Poodle'. The last section of this Standard on the Red Poodle is of particular historic interest. I originally thought that 'Red' referred to the Apricot we know today, but my research in the early Stud Books revealed both 'Apricot' and 'Red' Poodles.

The Perfect Black Poodle

General Appearance: That of a strong, active and very intelligent dog; well built, and profusely coated with curls or long ropey 'cords'.

Head: Long; the skull large and with plenty of room for brain power; wide between the ears and a slight peak; the parts over the eyes well arched; the whole thickly covered with curls or cords.

Muzzle: Long (but not 'snipey'), strong, square, and deep; the 'stop' should be defined, but not to a very great extent. The teeth should be perfectly level, strong and white.

Eyes: Small, dark, and bright, with a very intelligent expression: they should be set at right angles with the line of the face.

Nose: Large, and perfectly black in colour, with wide, open nostrils.

Ears: Very long, close to the cheek,

low set on, and well covered with long ringlets or 'cords'.

Neck: Well proportioned, and very strong to admit of the head being carried high and with dignity.

Chest: Fairy deep, but not to wide; strong, and well covered with muscles.

Legs: Forelegs, perfectly straight, very musucular and 'set on racing lines'. They should be long enough to raise the body well from the ground, but without legginess. Hind legs very muscular, fairly bent, with the hocks well let down.

Feet: Large, strong, and rather wide, but standing well on the toes and of good shape; the nails perfectly black, and the pads capacious and hard.

Back: Short, with body well ribbed up; the loins very strong and muscular, but without fat.

Tail: Carried at an angle of 45 degrees, having long ringlets or cords, hanging down.

Coat: Thick and strong. If corded, hanging in long, ropey 'cords'. If curly, the curls close and thick.

Weight: Large: 60lb; *(27kg)*: medium: 40lb; *(18kg)*: small: 20lb; *(9kg)* and under.

The Perfect Red Poodle

All the foregoing points hold good for this variety with the following exceptions:

Eyes: Yellow, and free from black rims round the eyelids.

Nose: Liver colour.

Nails: Liver colour.

Back: The ticks (spots) on back should be red or liver, and the whole body should be free from black ticks.

Coat colour and texture

Finally, examine the coat for both colour and texture. Black puppies if they are going to be a good black on maturity should have a puppy coat of jet black. Browns and Apricots usually fade as they mature, so they must have a really dark colour at this stage. Silvers are born black but by eight weeks the colour under the feet and around the eyes will be evident.

The pigment on the nose, lips and eyerims on Creams and Whites must be black, with black toenails desirable. A Brown Poodle should have a dark liver nose, lips, eyerims and toenails. Blacks, Silvers and Blues should have black noses, lips, eyerims and toenails. Apricots with dark eyes have black noses, lips and eyerims; with deep amber eyes, they have liver noses, lips and eyerims.

The texture of the puppy coat is rather difficult to judge, but a thin sparse coat should be avoided. Look for a thick, dense, fairly long coat with a slight curl at the roots.

Weight and height

A Standard at eight weeks should weigh approximately 10½ lbs (4.8kg) and should be 10-11in (25.5-28cm) in height with plenty of growth in the bone, looking on the whole rather ungainly and overheaded. A Miniature weighs approximately 5lbs (2.3kg) and Toys 3lbs (1.4kg) at the same age.

A good looking puppy at eight weeks will usually be good on maturity, but all sizes have their 'ugly' stage at between five to nine months, Miniatures at this age often seem to look leggy, Standards not big enough and Toys a little unbalanced.

TRAINING FOR THE SHOW RING

Most of the basic training for the Standard, Miniature and Toy Poodles is the same, with the following differences. The Standard does not require any training to stand quietly on the table while being examined by the judge. It will need to be taught to stand and to

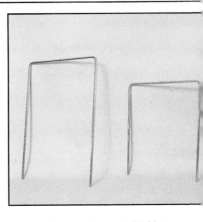

Above: *Two standard metal bridge measures, the 15in (38cm) for Miniatures, and the 11in (28cm) for the Toy Poodles.*

Right: *An excellent example of training a young puppy to stand correctly for its show career.*

lay down on the table for grooming, but in the show ring it will always be examined while standing quietly on the ground.

Measuring

The 'measure' is only used on the Miniature and Toy.

The Kennel Club Standard calls for a maximum height which should be under 38cm (15in) for Miniatures (US: 15ins or under and over 10ins), and under 28cm (11ins) for Toys (US: 10ins or under), measured at the shoulders. The KC Championship Show Regulations state: 'Before it receives a Class award or Reserve at a show, Miniature and Toy Poodles must be measured with the appropriate measure on a hard, level, non-slippery surface by the judge making this award'. To carry out the measuring the Show Committee must also provide a fixed, bridge-type, metal measure of 15in (38cm) and 11in (28cm) respectively.

The measuring nearly always takes place on a table and is routine during the judge's examination. Therefore, in addition to the

following training procedures, it is necessary to get your Miniature or Toy Poodle accustomed to the metal measure being placed over their shoulders without shying away. This is quite a simple exercise which they will quickly accept if, from a young age, they are placed on a table and the measure put quickly over their shoulders daily.

Show position

To obtain the correct show position, hold the head of the Poodle and place the front legs with both feet quite straight turning neither in nor out. A dog with the correct conformation, if slightly lifted from the ground by its head, will drop back down to the ground without any need for adjustment. After the front is correctly placed, if necessary adjust the rear legs so that they are parallel and not too close together. Now, hold the lead fairly taut with the collar just behind the ears, keeping the dog's head upright with your left hand ready to adjust the tail to its correct position if it begins to flag.

The earlier the young puppy

starts its training for the part it must play as a show dog, the quicker it will learn. As soon as the puppy has settled in its new home, start by standing it on a table. Go over its head, body and legs. Gently examine its mouth and teeth and stroke its back, praising all the time. Place the dog in a show position, giving the command 'Stay'. Reward with a tit-bit, no matter how short the 'stay'.

The first lesson should always be short, no more than a minute, with the 'stay' position held quite briefly. This routine must be practised every day always using the same procedure but increasing the 'stay' a little longer each time. Always give a reward which should be something the dog really enjoys and is never given at any other time: a piece of cheese or a piece of well cooked liver or chicken. I prefer cheese which is dry and always available.

The Triangle

In training your Poodle to move well in the show ring, it is a good idea to set up a temporary ring in your garden. The dog must always be between you and the judge, so always have the loosely-held lead in your left hand. Most judges require dogs to move in a triangle, enabling them to assess the dog's movement when they are moving away, sideways and coming towards the judge. But occasionally, the judge requires a straight walk up and down the ring. If so, at the turn do not alter your walk. Just move round in a small 'U' turn without breaking the dog's stride. If you stop and turn the dog round suddenly, it can lose its stride and momentum, and move badly on its return to the judge.

Practise the Triangle in the garden, encouraging the dog with your voice. Keep its head upright. If it tries to sniff the ground, pat under the chin and a firm 'no' must be used until the dog understands what you require, when praise and a tit-bit are its reward.

The mouth

Get as many people as possible to 'go over' your dog on the table especially strangers, which will accustom it to the various methods judges use on examination. Do not forget to ask them to look at the dog's teeth. This is done by gently parting the lips with one hand placed on the lower jaw and the other on the top jaw. The fingers are used to gently push down the bottom lip and raise the top lip. This is all that is required to ascertain the Poodle's correct bite and number of teeth; there is no necessity to open the jaw itself.

SHOW SYSTEMS

Having prepared and trained your poodle for its first outing into the exciting world of dog shows, you will need to study the whole range of shows available to you and their various entry requirements. Dog shows are run under the auspices of national kennel clubs, and the nature of the shows themselves and the rules and regulations governing them vary in a number of aspects from country to country (addresses of kennel clubs listed in the Appendix).

The groups

Some shows are specific to one breed (or variety of breed), called specialty shows; others encompass all breeds. At the all-breed or Championship shows, once the Best of Breed has been awarded for each individual breed competing in the show, these winners must compete in their 'group' before they can be considered for the top award, Best in Show. In the UK, all breeds are divided into six groups, and all three varieties of Poodle are judged in the Utility group. In the US, where the group system of judging is also used, the Standard and Miniature Poodles are placed in the Non-sporting group, an equivalent group to the UK Utility, but the Toy Poodle is placed in the Toy group.

THE UK SHOW SYSTEM

Types of show

The various types of show in the UK are detailed below. It would be wise for a novice exhibitor with a young dog to choose a local or small show, graduating to the larger Open and Championship shows as the puppy matures.

Exemption show This is usually held in aid of a charitable cause and is the only dog show where unregistered dogs may be exhibited. These are usually carefree and informal occasions held more for fun than serious competition, and as they always have four classes for pedigree dogs, often including a puppy class, this is an ideal show for a puppy's first outing.

Sanction show This is confined to members of the canine club or association holding the show. Once again, if you are a member of a club, they are great shows for puppies.

Primary show This is very similar to a Sanction Show, again restricted to breed club members and also excellent for puppies.

Limited show This is restricted to members of clubs or societies or to exhibitors within a specified, geographic area.

Open shows These are usually fairly large shows which are open to all exhibitors but without any Challenge Certificates on offer.

Championships shows These are the most important events in the dog show calendar. At these shows, the Kennel Club Challenge Certificates are on offer. The number of CCs allocated to a breed are based on the annual number of dogs registered at the Kennel Club. Hence, the numerically larger breeds are awarded more CCs in the year than their less popular counterparts.

Awards

Challenge Certificate (CC) This is awarded to the Best Dog and Best Bitch in each breed, but only when, as is stated on the Certificate given to the owner and signed by the Judge, 'in his opinion the dog is worthy of the title of Champion'. A judge not of this opinion can still award Best of Sex (Dog or Bitch) but must withhold the CC.

Reserve Challenge Certificate This is awarded to the Reserve Best of Sex. If the CC winner is disqualified, the Reserve Best of Sex is awarded the CC.

Champion A dog attains the title of Champion when it has won all three CCs at three Championship Shows under three different judges providing one CC is awarded when the dog is over 12 months old. All judges, before being passed to award these Certificates, are assessed by the Kennel Club for their experience, knowledge and achievements in the breed they are to judge.

Junior Warrant This may be awarded, by application to the Kennel Club, for any dog which has amassed 25 points before the age of 18 months. Points are awarded as follows: one point for a first prize at an Open show, and three points awarded for a first prize at a Championship show where Challenge Certificates are on offer for the breed.

Classes

The following is a definition of classes held at Open and Championship shows, taken from the Kennel Club Regulations for the Definition of Classes (reproduced by kind permission of the Kennel

Below: *Five magnificent Standard Poodles are briefly relaxing in the show ring before the judge begins his or her inspection.*

Club). These regulations are printed in all show schedules and should be studied carefully before entering your dog in any show. The term 'dog' in this context applies to both dogs and bitches. At most Championship shows, classes are duplicated for each sex, ie Puppy Dog, Puppy Bitch, etc. At the Open and smaller shows, these classes are usually mixed with dogs and bitches judged in the same class.

Minor puppy For dogs of six and not exceeding nine calendar months of age on the first day of the show.

Puppy For dogs of six and not exceeding twelve calendar months of age on the first day of the Show.

Junior For dogs of six and not exceeding 18 calendar months of age on the first day of the Show.

Maiden For dogs which have not won a Challenge Cerrtificate or a First Prize at an Open or Championship Show (Puppy, Special Puppy, Minor Puppy and special Minor Puppy classes excepted).

Novice For dogs which have not won a Challenge Certificate or three or more First Prizes at Open and Championship Shows (Puppy, Special Puppy, Minor Puppy and Special Minor Puppy classes excepted).

Tyro For dogs which have not won a Challenge Certificate or five or more First Prizes at Open and Championship Shows (Puppy, Special Puppy, Minor Puppy and Special Minor Puppy classes excepted).

Debutant For dogs which have not won a Challenge Certificate or a First Prize at a Championship Show (Puppy, Special Puppy, Minor Puppy and Special Minor Puppy classes excepted).

Undergraduate For dogs which have not won a Challenge Certificate or three or more First Prizes at Championship Shows (Puppy, Special Puppy, Minor Puppy and Special Minor Puppy classes excepted).

Graduate For dogs which have not won a Challenge Certificate or four

or more First Prizes at Championship Shows in Graduate, Post Graduate, Minor Limit, Mid Limit, Limit and Open Classes, whether restricted or not.

Minor Limit For dogs which have not won two Challenge Certificates or three or more First Prizes in all at Championship shows in Minor Limit, Mid Limit, Limit and Open Classes, confined to the breed, whether restricted or not, at shows where Challenge Certificates were offered for the breed.

Mid Limit For dogs which have not won three Challenge Certificates or five or more First Prizes in all at Championship shows in Mid Limit, Limit and Open Classes, confined to the breed, whether restricted or not, at shows where CCs were offered for the breed.

Limit For dogs which have not won three Challenge Certificates under three different judges or seven or more First Prizes in all, at Championship Shows in Limit and Open Classes, confined to the breed, whether restricted or not, at shows where Challenge Certificates were offered for the breed.

Open For all dogs of the breeds for which the class is provided and eligible for entry at the Show.

In addition, there are Veteran classes for dogs over five years of age, Brace and Team classes for pairs and teams of dogs, and sweepstake classes, open to Veteran, Brace, Team, Stud Dog, Brood Bitch and Breeders Classes, in which some of the fees may be awarded as prize money.

Registration
To exhibit at any show run under the jurisdiction of the Kennel Club, your puppy must be registered at the Kennel Club.

Forthcoming Shows
The two weekly dog papers available in the UK, 'Our Dogs' and 'Dog World', carry a comprehensive list of all forthcoming shows, giving the venue, date, type of show with the breeds allocated, judges, classes and the show secretary's address

and telephone number. As schedules are only sent to the previous year's exhibitors, it will be necessary for you to apply for a schedule by post or by telephone. As show dates are always planned well in advance, you will have ample time to study the schedule and choose your classes.

Fill in the entry form taking care that all the details are correct and that the declaration is also signed correctly. Make sure you do not forget to enclose the entry fee. At the same time, write on the cover of your schedule the name of the dog and the classes you have entered. It is easy to forget these important details once the entry has been posted.

THE CONTINENTAL SHOW SYSTEM

In Europe, all dog shows are governed by regulations laid down by the FCI (Fédération Cynologique Internationale), with small national differences. Each country also has its own Kennel Club.

Basically there are two main types of show: championship shows and small, informal, fun shows, usually held by breed clubs.

Judging
Judging takes the form of a written critique on each exhibit, graded

Above: *Three beautiful Miniatures — two Black and one Silver — all in perfect condition ready for exhibition in the show ring.*

excellent, very good, good or sufficient. This report is usually written on the spot and passed to the exhibitor. Judging, therefore, can be a lengthy process, but there are far fewer shows in Europe as well as fewer exhibitions than in either the US or UK.

Classes
Usually, classes are limited to Youth, Open and Championship, although additional classes are allowed. Periodically, there are Brace and Team classes. The Youth class limits exhibitors by age, usually 9-24 months.

Awards
Only dogs awarded an excellent grading can be considered for the Best of Sex award. In some countries, the excellent grading is excluded from the Youth class.

Best of Breed is a fairly rare award in Europe. Consequently, there cannot be any group or Best in Show judging. Exhibitors deemed to be of outstanding merit over and above the excellent grading may be awarded the CACIB (Cerificat d'Aptitude au

109

Championat International de Beauté) or the CAC Certificat d'Aptitude au Championat). The CACIB can only be awarded at international championship shows.

To become a champion, a dog must be awarded three certificates (CACIB or CAC) under two different judges, with at least a 12-month interval between the first and last certificates. These certificates can be won in any country affiliated to the FCI.

THE US SHOW SYSTEM

US Breed Specialty shows

The three varieties of Poodle are shown separately. The Best of Variety Toy, Miniature and Standard compete against each other for Best of Breed. Within the varieties are six classes, each class having four placements, from first to fourth. The classes are divided between dogs, which are shown first, and bitches, shown after the dogs. First place dogs compete again for Winners Dog, as do the first place bitches for Winners Bitch. Only Winners Dog and Winners Bitch may be awarded Championship points. The Winners will then compete against the 'Specials' — Champions of record — for Best of Variety.

Classes

The classes at specialty and all-breed shows are primarily the same.

Puppy For dogs of 6-12 months of age. The class may be divided into 6-9 months and 9-12 months.
Novice This class is for dogs at least six months of age that have not won a class except Puppy, and have not won more than three times in Novice.
Bred by exhibitor In this class, dogs must be shown by the breeder or co-breeder.
American bred For dogs of six months of age or older bred in the US.
Open For dogs at least six months of age, usually entered by more mature dogs. An imported dog must be entered in this class.

Specials For Champions of record. Both dogs and bitches are shown together in this class with the Winners Dog and Winners Bitch.

US All-Breed shows

At all-breed shows, the same classes apply within the varieties. The Best of Variety is shown again in its group, ie Toy Poodles in the Toy group, Miniatures and Standards in the Non-Sporting group. There are four placements in each of the seven groups. The first place winners from each group go on to compete for Best in Show. An all-breed show, with entry of around 2,000 dogs, will eventually come down to the best of seven dogs: the winners of the Hound, Sporting, Working, Terrier, Toy, Non-Sporting and Herding groups.

Matches

AKC sanctioned matches for pure-bred dogs competing on an informal basis are given by specialty and all-breed clubs. No Championship points are awarded. These events provide an excellent opportunity for clubs, exhibitors, stewards and those wishing to become judges to gain experience needed for licensed shows. Sometimes a club will give a puppy match, limiting the entry to dogs of 3-12 months of age. This is a good time to socialize your new puppy and gain some show-ring experience.

Obedience and Junior Showmanship classes may be offered at sanctioned or fun matches as well.

Champions

A dog or bitch must gain 15 points under at least three different judges to become a Champion. Championship points are awarded to Winners Dog and Winners Bitch. The number of points awarded at each show will vary according to geographic location and the number of dogs entered. Each Champion must have won at least two major point shows. Both 'majors' must be won under different judges. These shows award a minimum of three points; no show will award more than five points.

YOUR FIRST SHOW

Preparations
Having decided on the date and venue for your first venture into the show ring, and with your Poodle in tip-top condition, you now have to prepare for the day itself. Keep a special 'show bag' packed with the following necessities: blanket for the bench or cage; a reliable collar; benching chain; water bowl; disinfectants for the bench; grooming equipment and show clip; paper tissues. Remember to feed your Poodle the evening before the show at the latest; the earlier you feed on the day before the show the better. This will lessen considerably the chance of the dog being sick during the journey to the show and, as the dog will be a little hungry, make it keener to obey your commands in anticipation of the tit-bit.

The major Championship shows in the UK provide benching or cages for all breeds. The benching is for the larger breeds, ie Standard and Miniature Poodles. The cages are provided for all Toy breeds including the Toy Poodle. These benches and cages are all numbered. For the Championship shows, you will have received by post, prior to the show, your exhibitor's pass combined with your removal order. This numbered pass is your bench and ring number. In other shows, you must check your number in the catalogue on arrival, which will correspond to the number on your bench (or carried on your armband in the US). Take care of the removal order; you will need this when you leave the show. This order is provided to prevent anyone but yourself from leaving the showground with your dog.

At the show site
As soon as you arrive at the show, collect your catalogue; the stand could be a long way from your bench. Find your bench or cage and give it a quick spray with disinfectant. Make your dog as comfortable as possible with its blanket. Make sure the dog is securely tethered by the right length of lead or chain; if too long the dog may jump down and choke itself. If a cage is provided, check that the fastenings are safe. You

Below: *A White Standard wins the Utility Group and becomes overall winner of the Kennel Club Junior Organisation Stakes at Crufts 1987.*

can provide added safety by tying a lead around the door.

Check your entry in the catalogue. If there are any discrepancies in the details, ie wrong date of birth, class or name, you will need to go to the show secretary's tent, where your entry form will be checked. If it is a printing error, all will be well. If, however, the mistake is your own, you will need to be governed by the secretary's ruling. Next, find out the approximate time your class will be judged and locate your ring.

After setting up your grooming table and unpacking your equipment, give your Poodle a slow and pleasant walk around the showground. This will give the dog the opportunity to get acclimatised to the noise and atmosphere, and also a chance to relieve itself.

Even after lengthy, professional preparation of your Poodle's coat prior to the show, it will still be necessary, after the journey, to allow yourself enough time at the show to give it a final thorough brush and comb. Take particular care of the top-knot, bracelets, ear fringes and pom-pom, thus adding the final touches.

In the ring
When it is nearly time for your class, walk slowly to your ring. When the class is called, enter quietly and collect your ring number which is distributed to all exhibitors by the steward. This number must be pinned to your dress or lapel in a prominent position where it can be easily seen by the judge and those at the ringside. In the US, an arm band bearing your number will be given to you before entering the ring, which is worn on the left arm. Stand in line with the other exhibitors leaving enough space for the exhibitor in front and behind you. Now set up your dog to look its very best. Make sure the front and back legs are in the correct position, with the head and tail well up. The previous training of 'stand and stay' will now be appreciated.

At this point, keep one eye on the judge and one on the dog. After the judge has walked down the line briefly examining all the exhibits, his or her attention will then be concentrated on the first exhibit. Now you can relax and praise your Poodle until the time comes for it to stand on the table for the judge's detailed examination. Never talk to the judge. If asked any questions, answer briefly. These questions are usually with regard to the dog's date of birth, so do memorize its exact age.

At the conclusion of this examination, the judge will instruct you how he or she wishes you to

---

Show tips

DOs	DON'Ts
Plan journey allowing ample time	Forget schedule or passes
Keep schedule and passes to hand	Be tense or nervous
Keep a towel in the car	Rush into the ring
Buy catalogue on arrival and check entries	Wear sloppy clothes or high heels
Offer dog a drink	Put yourself between the dog and the judge
Take it for a leisurely walk	Drop tit-bits in the ring
Give a final grooming	Use squeaky toys in the ring
Enter your class slowly	Walk too close to the exhibitor in front
Have the dog on your left	Let your dog interfere with others
Watch and listen to the judge	Blame your dog if unplaced
If placed in the first three, stay until dismissed, congratulate the winner and thank the judge.	Leave dog on bench unattended for too long
Be a good loser	Lose your removal card
	Forget there is always another show

move, in order to assess the dog's movement. As mentioned on page 105, this is usually a triangle which enables the judge to see side movement as well as the front and back. The judge will tell you exactly in which direction he or she wishes this to be executed. With a word of encouragement to your dog and keeping it on the left side on a fairly loose lead, walk smartly with confidence. At the completion of the judge's scrutiny, return in line with the other exhibitors. Now you will be able to make a fuss of your dog, which can relax until the judge has seen all the exhibits, when once again set up the dog to look its best in readiness for the judge's final selection.

The line-up
Placings of first, second, third and fourth (sometimes fifth in the UK) are the usual awards. If you have won one of these placings, stay in line until the Steward has given you your card. If placed in the first three, wait until the judge gives you permission to leave, then thank the judge, congratulate any exhibitor

placed above you and quietly leave the ring.

As already stated, dog shows vary greatly in size, but at all these shows, whether large or small, you will be able to talk and learn from other breeders and exhibitors, and in addition enjoy a day out amongst people dedicated to the future and well being of our friend the dog.

CRUFTS DOG SHOW

It can be safely said that Crufts Dog Show, held annually in London, is the world's most famous dog show.

Charles Crufts with great flair and ability arranged dog shows from the 1870s but is was not until 1891 that the first dog show to be called 'Crufts' was held at the Royal Agricultural Hall Islington, its full title, 'Crufts Great International Dog Show'. Mrs Crufts in her 'Dog Book' gives the following information on this first Crufts: 'There were 2,000 dogs, 2,500 entries, 473 classes and 20 judges . . . With the exception of the years 1918-1920, Crufts Show at Islington became internationally famous'.

In 1942 Mrs Crufts reached an agreement with the Kennel Club that, providing the name 'Crufts' was adhered to, the Kennel Club would be responsible for the Shows in the future. The first Crufts Dog

Below: *No matter how well prepared at home, the final touches are always necessary at the show. This lovely White Poodle obviously enjoys the attention.*

Show under the auspices of the Kennel Club was held at Olympia on October 14-15 1948. 4,273 dogs making 9,412 entries filled 918 classes. The public response was incredible: 50,000 visitors from home and abroad attended the show.

Poodles at Crufts

The Standard and the Miniature Poodle were the only two sizes recognised in 1948; Miss Lavinia Graham Weall judged them both. In Standards, Ch Ravenslea Phantom of Toytown, a Silver owned by Mr G Sand, bred by Mrs Sine Fordham, won the Dog CC with Ch Peaslake Fairey Firefly, another Sivler, bred and owned by Mrs E Hilliard, winning the Bitch CC. In Miniatures, the Dog CC went to Ch Top Hat of Piperscroft, a Black, owned and bred by Mrs G L Boyd, and the Bitch CC was awarded to Ch Braeval Brioche, another Black, owned and bred by Mrs P Austin Smith.

Since 1928, when for the first time a Best in Show award was instigated, four Poodles have won this prestigious award, two Standards and two Toys. In 1955, Best in Show was awarded to a Brown Standard Poodle, Ch Tzigane Aggri of Nashend, owned by Joan Eddie and bred by Mrs A Proctor; in 1966 an Apricot Toy Poodle, Oakington Puckshill Amber Sunblush, owned by Clare Coxall bred by Mrs M Dobson; in 1982, nearly 20 years later, another Toy, Ch Grayco Hazlenut, a Brown, bred and owned by Mrs Howard; and in 1985, the Black Standard, Ch Montravia Tommy Gun bred by Clare Coxall and owned by Miss Marita Gibbs.

The magic of Crufts has continued with the entries rising rapidly every year. So much so that in 1967 the Kennel Club Crufts Committee brought in restrictions. In that year any Standard, Miniature or Toy Poodle who had won a first, second or third prize in the breed classes at a Championship Show between January and December the previous year, or carried the title of Champion, were thus qualified for Crufts. Since that time, year after year entries have continued to rise. Therefore, with the limited space available, even more qualifications were imposed until today for a Poodle to be eligible for entry at Crufts the qualifications shown in the box are essential.

Below: *The International Finals of Junior Handling being judged at Crufts 1987. Frances Hurley from Jersey won 3rd prize handling this White Miniature Poodle.*

Entry Qualifications

1. Any Poodle with the title of Champion
2. Any Poodle entered, or qualified, for entry in the Kennel Club Stud Book by the closing date for the Crufts entries (a first, second or third prize awarded in Limit or Open class at a Championship Show where CCs are on offer, or an award of a CC or Reserve CC, entitles your Poodle for an entry in the Stud Book)
3. Plus a win of a first prize in any of the following classes for the breed: Minor Puppy; Puppy; Junior; Post Graduate
4. A win of a first prize in a breed Class at Crufts the previous year.

Above: *Ch Aedean Twice as Nice photographed winning Reserve in the Utility Group at Crufts 1987. A Lovely, well-balanced Toy Poodle superbly presented.*

Below: *Ch Montravia Tommy Gun with the Crufts Trophy 1985. Tommy Gun holds the record in the three sizes of Poodles with a total of 53 Challenge Certificates.*

Appendix

Abbreviations

AI	Artificial insemination
AKC	American Kennel Club
ANKC	Australian National Kennel Club
AOC	Any other colour
AVNSC	Any Variety Not Separately Classified
B	Bitch
BIS	Best in Show
BOB	Best of Breed
BOS	Best Opposite Sex
CAC	Certificat d'aptitude au Championnat de Beauté
CACIB	Certificat d'aptitude au Championnat International de Beauté
CC	Challenge Certificate
CD	Companion Dog
CDX	Companion Dog Excellent
Ch	Champion
CKC	Canadian Kennel Club
D	Dog
FCI	Federation Cynologique Internationale
Int Ch	International Champion
IPC	International Poodle Club
JW	Junior Warrant
KC	Kennel Club (UK)
LKA	Ladies Kennel Association
LOF	Livre des Origines Francais (French Stud Book)
LOSH	Livre Origines St Hubert (Belgian Stud Book)
NAF	Name applied for
Nordic Ch	Nordic Champion
OBCh	Obedience Champion
P	Puppy
PRA	Progressive Retinal Atrophy
Res CC	Reserve Challenge Certificate
S	(Sieger) German Champion
TAF	Transfer applied for
WS	(Weltsieger) World Champion (Germany)

Useful Addresses

Kennel Clubs
Australia Australian National Kennel Council, Royal Show Grounds, Ascot Vale, Victoria
Belgium Societe Royale Saint-Hubert, Avenue de l'Armee 25, B-1040, Brussels
Canada Canadian Kennel Club, 2150 Bloor Street West, Toronto M6S 1M8, Ontario
France Societie Centrale Canine, 215 Rue St Denis, 75083 Paris, Cedex 02
Germany Verband ffur das Deutsche Hundewesen (VDH), Postfach 1390, 46 Dortmund
Holland Raad van Beheer op Kynologisch Gebied in Nederland, Emmalaan 16, Amsterdam, Z
Ireland Irish Kennel Club, 23 Earlsfort Terrace, Dublin 2
Italy Ente Nazionale Della Cinofilia Italiana, Viale Premuda, 21 Milan
New Zealand New Zealand Kennel Club, Private Bag, Porirua, New Zealand
Spain Real Sociedad Central de Fomento de las razas en Espana, Los Madrazo 20, Madrid 14
United Kingdom The Kennel Club, 1-4 Clarges Street, London W1Y 8AB
United States of America American Kennel Club, 51 Madison Avenue, New York, NY 10010; The United Kennel Club Inc, 100 East Kilgore Road, Kalamazoo, MI 49001-5598

Glossary of dog terminology

Affix:	The word used by an owner of a kennel which, when registering a puppy at the Kennel Club, is written in front of the puppy's name to indicate the puppy has been bred by the owner. No one else may use the same word.
Almond eye:	The eye set in an almond-shaped surround.
Anorchid:	Male animal without testicles.
Anus:	Anterior opening under the tail.
Angulation:	Angle formed by the bones, mainly the shoulder, forearm, stifle and hock.
Backline:	Topline of dog from neck to tail.
Balance:	Correctly proportioned animal with correct balance, with one part in regard to another.
Bands:	Clipped area on back legs.
Barrel ribs:	Ribs which are so rounded as to interfere with the elbow action.
Bitch:	Female dog.
Brisket:	The forepart of the body below the chest between the forelegs.
Brood bitch:	Female used for breeding.
Brace:	Two dogs of the same breed.
Bracelets:	Puffs on front and back legs.
Brace Class:	A class for two exhibits of the same breed owned by one person.
Canine:	Animal of the genus canis which includes dogs, foxes, wolves and jackals.
Canines:	The four large teeth in the front of the mouth, two upper and two lower next to incisors.
Castrate:	To surgically remove the testes of a male.
China eye:	A clear blue eye.
Chiselling:	On a Poodle, a well-chiselled foreface refers to clean cut below the eyes, not falling away or protruding, with skin tight giving a fine appearance and strong foreface.
Close coupled:	A dog comparatively short from ribs to pelvis.
Coarse:	Skull heavy in bone, wedge-shaped in muzzle.
Conformation:	The structure and form of the framework of a dog in comparison with the requirements of the Breed Standard.
Cow hocked:	Hocks turned inwards.
Croup:	The back part of the back above the hind legs.
Cryptorchid:	A male dog with neither testicle descended.
Cull:	To eliminate unwanted puppies.
Dam:	Mother of the puppies.
Dew claw:	Extra claw on the inside lower portion of legs.
Dishface:	Nose higher at the end than in the middle or at the stop.
Distemper teeth:	Pitted or discoloured teeth as the result of distemper or other diseases.
Dock:	To shorten the tail by cutting.
Double coat:	Undercoat plus outer longer coat.
Down in pastern:	Weak or faulty pastern. (Metacarpus) ie forelegs bent at pastern.
Down faced:	Tip of nose below level of stop.
Drive:	Good thrust of rear quarters.
Dudley nose:	Brown or light brown nose.
Elbow:	The joint at the top of the forelegs.
Fiddle front:	A crooked front out at elbow, pasterns close and feet turned out.
Femur:	The large heavy bone of the thigh between the pelvis and stifle joint.
Forearm:	Front leg between elbow and pastern.
Hackney action:	Front feet lifted high in action.
Hare foot:	A long narrow foot — a fault in the Poodle.
Haw:	A third eyelid at the inside corner of the eye.
Heat:	An alternative word for 'season' in bitches.
Height:	Vertical measurements from withers to ground.
Hock:	Lower joint of the hind-legs.
Humerus:	Bone of the upper arm.
In-breeding:	The mating of closely related dogs of the same standard.
Incisors:	Upper and lower front teeth between the canines.

Poodle Clubs

UK The Poodle Council (a representative body of all Poodle clubs in the UK), Mrs S M Coupe, 'San Juan', Doddinghurst Road, Doddinghurst, Brentwood, Essex; British Toy Poodle Club, Mrs S Cox, White Oak, Ducks Hill Road, Northwood, Middlesex; International Poodle Club, Mrs K Rees, The Well House, Binfield Heath, Henley-on-Thames, Oxon
US Poodle Club of Long Island, 203 Fairfield Avenue, Carle Place, New York; Washington Poodle Club, 1225 Potomac Street, NW Washington DC; Poodle Club of Southern California 419, North Leland Street, West Covina, California; Heart of America Poodle Club, Route 1 Box 101, Dearborn, Missouri; The William Penn Poodle Club, 607 Meadow Lane, Oreland, Pennsylvania

General

UK Groomers Association, Uplands, 151 Pampisford Road, South Croydon, Surrey CR2 6DE; National Dog Owners' Association 39-41 North Road, Islington, London N7; Canine Studies Institute, London Road, Bracknell, Berks RG12; Pet Food Manufacturers' Association, 6 Catherine Street, London WC2B 5JJ
US American Veterinary Medical Association, 930 North Meacham Road, Schaumburg, Illinois 60196; National Dog Groomers Association, PO Box 101, Clark, Pennsylvania 16113; Owner Handler Association of America, 583 Knoll Court, Seaford, New York 11783; Pet Food Institute, 1101 Conecticut Avenue NW, Washington DC 20036

Further Reading

The Inheritance of Coat Colour in Dogs, Clarence C Little, Comstock Cornell, New York
Practical Dog Breeding and Genetics, Eleanor Frankling, Popular Dogs, London
Breeding From Your Poodle, Sheldon & Lockwood, W & G Foyle, London
The Conformation of the Dog, R H Smyth, Popular Dogs, London
Canine Terminology, H Spira, Harper & Row, Sydney
Understanding Your Dog, Michael W Fox, The Anchor Press Ltd, UK
Dog Steps, R P Elliot, Howell Book House, New York
The Book of the Poodle, T H Tracy, Harvill, London
The Poodle, C Bowring & A Munroe, Popular Dogs, London
The Complete Poodle, Lydia Hopkins, Delinger, New York
Poodles in Particular, A L ROgers, Orange Judd, New York
Poodles in America, W H Ivens, Poodle Club of America, New York
The Miniature Poodle, P H Prince, Nicholson & Watson, Surrey
The Standard Poodle, S Walne, K & R Books, UK
The Complete Poodle Clipping and Grooming Book, Shirlee Kalstone, Howell Book House, New York

Acknowledgments

We wish to thank the following for their help with the photography: Clare Coxhall, Pat Rose, Brian Johns of Petcetera etc, Suzanne Ruiz and A. Neaverson & Sons Ltd.

Layback:	The angle of the shoulder blade compared with the vertical.
Leather:	The flap of the ear.
Level bite:	The upper and lower teeth edge to edge.
Line breeding:	The mating of related dogs within a line or family to a common ancestor, ie dog to grand-dam or bitch to grand-sire.
Loaded:	Superfluous muscle.
Loin:	Either side of the vertebrae column between the last rib and hip bone.
Maiden:	An unmated bitch, or a dog or bitch that has never won a first prize.
Mane:	Long profuse coat covering the chest, body and ribs on a Poodle.
Mate:	The sex act between the dog and bitch.
Monorchid:	A male animal with only one testicle in the scrotum.
Muzzle:	The head in front of the eyes, including nose, nostril and jaws.
Molars:	Rear teeth.
Molera:	Incomplete ossification of the skull.
Occiput:	The rear of the skull.
Oestrum:	The period during which a bitch has her menstrual flow and can be mated.
Out at elbow:	Elbows turning out from the body.
Out at shoulder:	Shoulder blades set too wide, hence just out from the body.
Overshot:	Front teeth (incisors) of the upper jaw overlap and do not touch the teeth of the lower jaw.
Pace:	The left foreleg and left hindleg advance in unison, then the right foreleg and right hindleg, causing a rolling movement.
Pastern:	Foreleg between the carpus and the digits.
Patella:	Knee cap composed of cartilage at the stifle joint.
Pelvis:	Set of bones attached to the end of the spinal column.
Pigeon-toed:	Forefeet inclined inwards.
Pom-pom:	Puff on the Poodle's tail.

Prefix:	Usually attached to the dog's name in order to identify it with a particular breeder.
Puppy:	A dog up to 12 months of age.
Quality:	Refinement and finesse.
Quarters:	The two hindlegs.
Register:	To record with the Kennel Club the dog's particulars.
Roach back:	A convex curvature of the back towards the loin.
Scissor bite:	The outside of the lower incisors touches the inner side of the upper incisors.
Second thigh:	The part of the hindquarters from stifle to hock.
Sire:	A dog's male parent.
Snipy:	Muzzle pointed and weak.
Spay:	To surgically remove the ovaries to prevent conception.
Splayed:	Flat feet.
Spring:	The roundness of ribs.
Standard:	A word picture of a breed in type and style.
Sternum:	The brisket or breast bone.
Stifle:	The hindleg above the hock.
Stop:	Indentation between the eyes.
Stud Book:	A record of pedigree, age, name, breeder and owner of all the recognised breeds.
Straight in shoulder:	The shoulder blades straight up and down as against laid back.
Thigh:	Hindquarters from hip to stifle.
Throatiness:	An excess of loose skin under the throat.
Topknot:	Long hair on head.
Topline:	The top outline of the Poodle in outline.
Undershot:	The front teeth of the lower jaw projecting or overlapping the front teeth of the upper jaw.
Upper arm:	The humerus or bone of the foreleg between shoulder blade and the forearm.
Vent:	The anal opening.
Weaving:	The crossing of the front or hindlegs when in action.
Whelp:	An unweaned puppy.
Whelping:	The act of giving birth.
Wry mouth:	Lower jaw does not line-up with upper jaw.

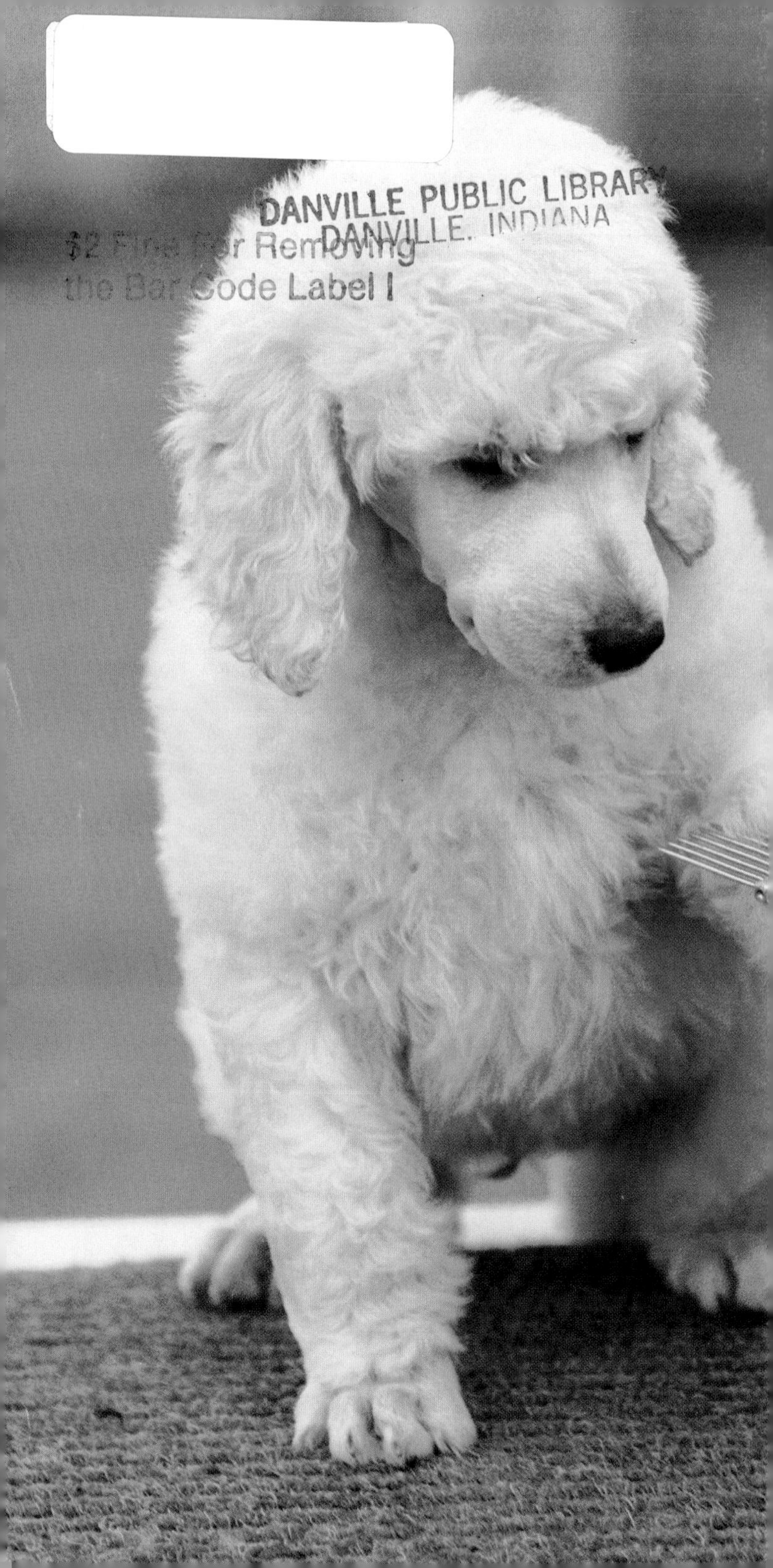